Black Historical Figures

ENTERTAINERS

Copyright © 2022 by Every Dollar Countz LLC
All rights reserved. This book or any portion thereof
may not be reproduced or used in any manner whatsoever
without the express written permission of the publisher
except for the use of brief quotations in a book review.

TABLE OF CONTENTS

43 CHADWICK BOSEMAN

99 LENA HORNE

131 ZENDAYA COLEMAN

3	Cicely Tyson	67	Hattie Mcdaniel	131	Zendaya Coleman
11	James Earl Jones	75	Spike Lee	139	LeVar Burton
19	Gail Fisher	83	Halle Berry	147	Diahann Carroll
27	Sidney Poitier	91	Tyler Perry	155	Harry Belafonte
35	Phylicia Rashad	99	Lena Horne	163	Angela Bassett
43	Chadwick Boseman	107	Nicholas Brothers	171	John Singleton
51	Oprah Winfrey	115	Misty Copeland	179	Viola Davis
59	Denzel Washington	123	Scott Joplin	187	Cabell Calloway
				195	Dorothy Dandridge

These Workbooks are geared to intrigue, inspire and motivate you to want to learn more about these Black Historical Figures(BHFs) and others. Also to do more research on your own. We know this isn't all the history of these individuals. We want you to do some of the research also. We try to be as accurate as possible during our research. If there are some stories or questions that aren't as stated, please contact us at info@wegonnalearntoday.com.

Cicely Tyson

Cicely Tyson

December 19, 1924 – January 28, 2021
ACTRESS

LEFT BLANK ON PURPOSE

Cicely Tyson

Cicely Tyson

Cicely Tyson

Cicely Tyson

Cicely Tyson

Cicely Tyson

Directions: read the bio below and answer the following questions.

Hi, my name is Cicely Tyson. I was born on December 19, 1924, in the Bronx, NY. I graduated from Charles Evans Hughes High School. I was discovered by a photographer who worked for Ebony magazine. In 1956, I started acting. My first film was Carib Gold. I appeared onstage for the first time in 1958 in the production "Dark of the Moon". In 1961, I made my television debut in the NBC series Frontiers of Faith. In 1963, I became the first African-American star in a TV drama in the series "East Side/West Side", in which I played the role of secretary Jane Foster. I only wanted to present positive images of Black women. I only seem to receive small roles until 1972, when I played the role of Rebecca Morgan in the film "Sounder". I was nominated for both the Academy Award and the Golden Globe Award for Best Actress for my work in "Sounder". But, I didn't win. However, I won the NSFC Best Actress and NBR Best Actress Awards for that film.

1. What was the name of my High School?
   A. Charles Evans Hughes High School
   B. Bronx High School for the Visual Arts
   C. Morris High School
2. What year did I start acting?
   A. 1950
   B. 1955
   C. 1956
3. I'm known as the person who?
   A. Would take any role
   B. Would take positive images of Black women
   C. Would only work on Broadway

Directions: Answer the questions, to solve the crossword puzzle. You can use the internet if you get stuck on any question.

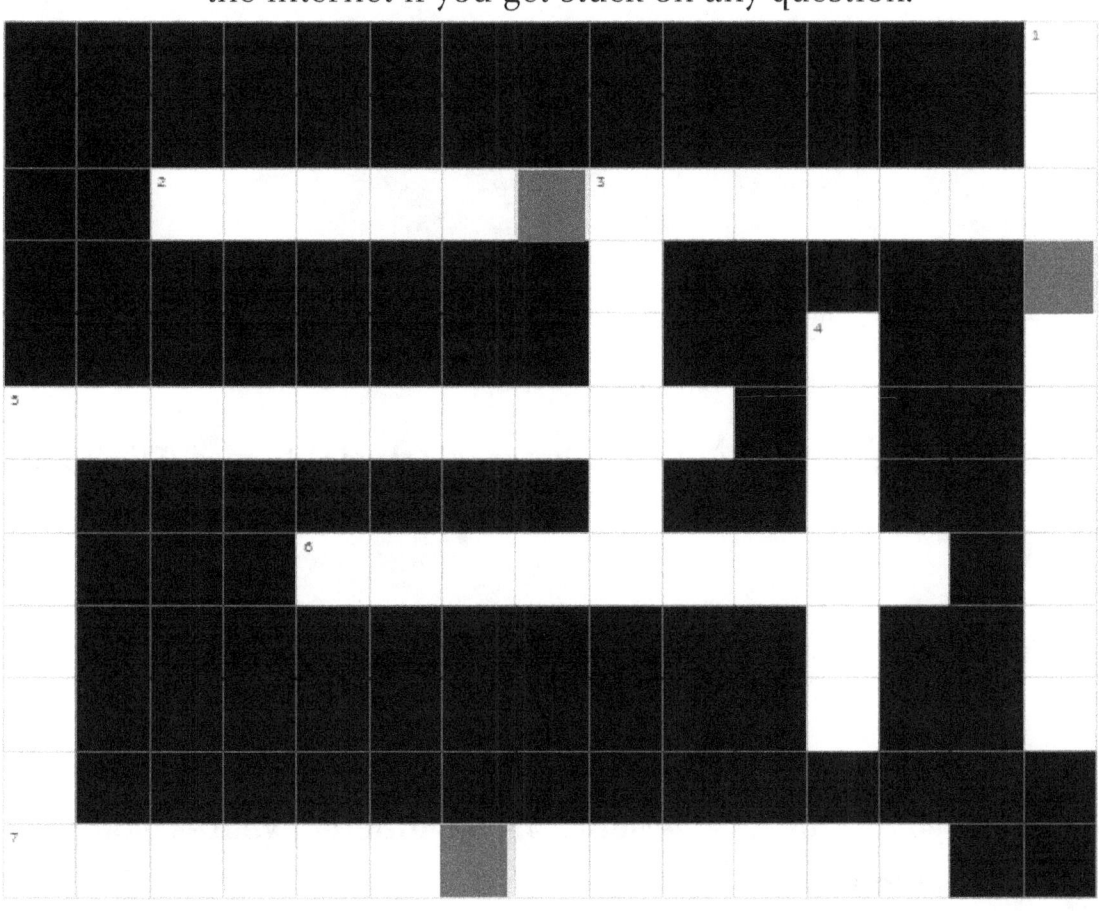

Across

2) Cicely served on the _____ of Harlem's national advisory board.
5) Cicely was inducted into the Black _____ Hall of Fame.
6) Cicely received a star on the _____ Walk of Fame in 1997.
7) Cicely has a _____ in New Jersey that was renamed after her as The Cicely Tyson School of Performing and Fine Arts.

Down

1) Cicely appeared in the 1961 Broadway play, _____, which recorded the longest performances in the history of Broadway.
3) After being gone for ___ years, Cicely won a Tony for Best Actress in the Broadway show "The Trip to Bountiful."
4) Cicely's _____, "Just as I Am," was published January 26, 2021 and she passed away two days later January 28, 2021.
5) Cicely was awarded the Presidential Medal of _____.

Directions: Read and answer the questions. These are your opinions so the answers will vary.

Who is your favorite entertainer and why?

What kind of entertainment do you enjoy most (music, movies, TV shows, etc.)?

Can you name some famous entertainers from different genres (comedy, drama, action, animation, etc.)?

Directions: Unscramble the words below about Cicely. See if you can get the bonus word.

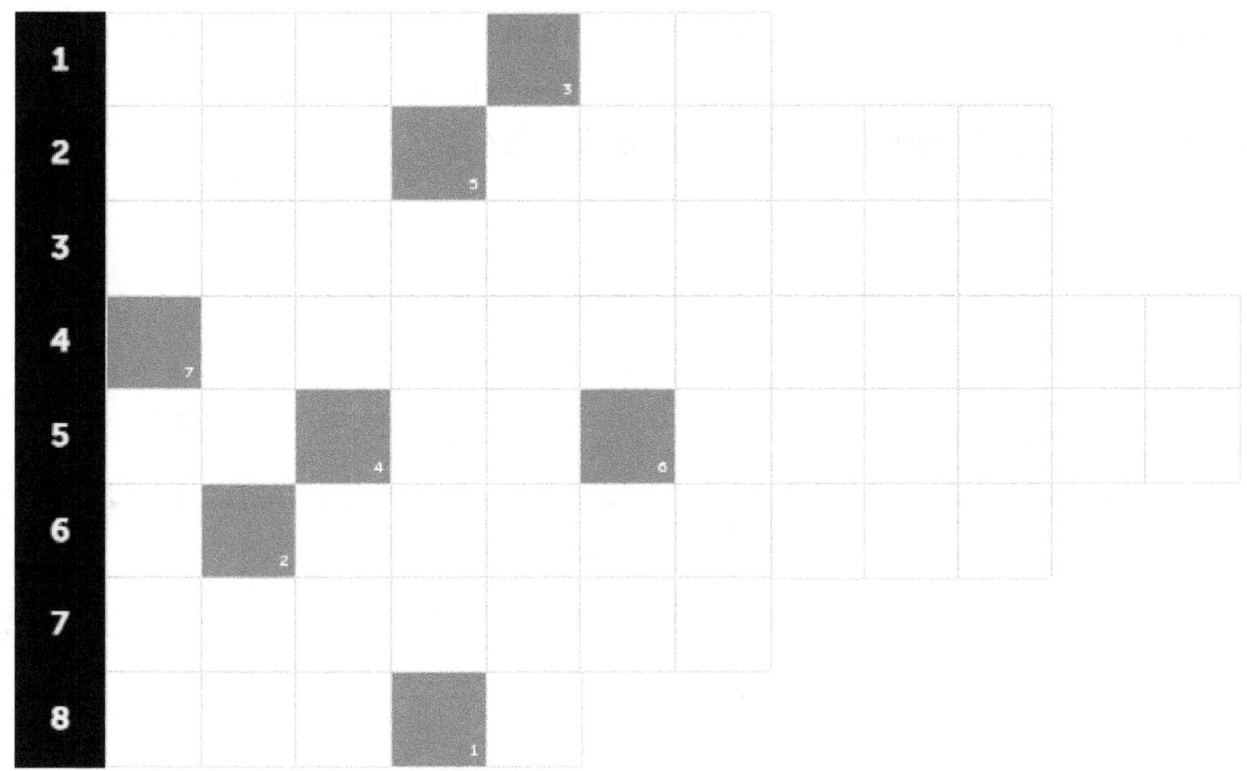

BONUS WORD

Unscramble Words

1) cearsts
2) siavmilsde
3) emrmsywada
4) yrdabpwadoea
5) vfmletolhfaa
6) mihtgneeag
7) endusro
8) toosr

Directions: This is the WGLT Challenge. Solve the cryptogram. As the puzzle solver, you need to find which number belongs to which character. And this can be pretty challenging! You will need to match the number with the letter. There are some letters given to you below. This will help you solve the other words and unlock more characters. **Good Luck.**

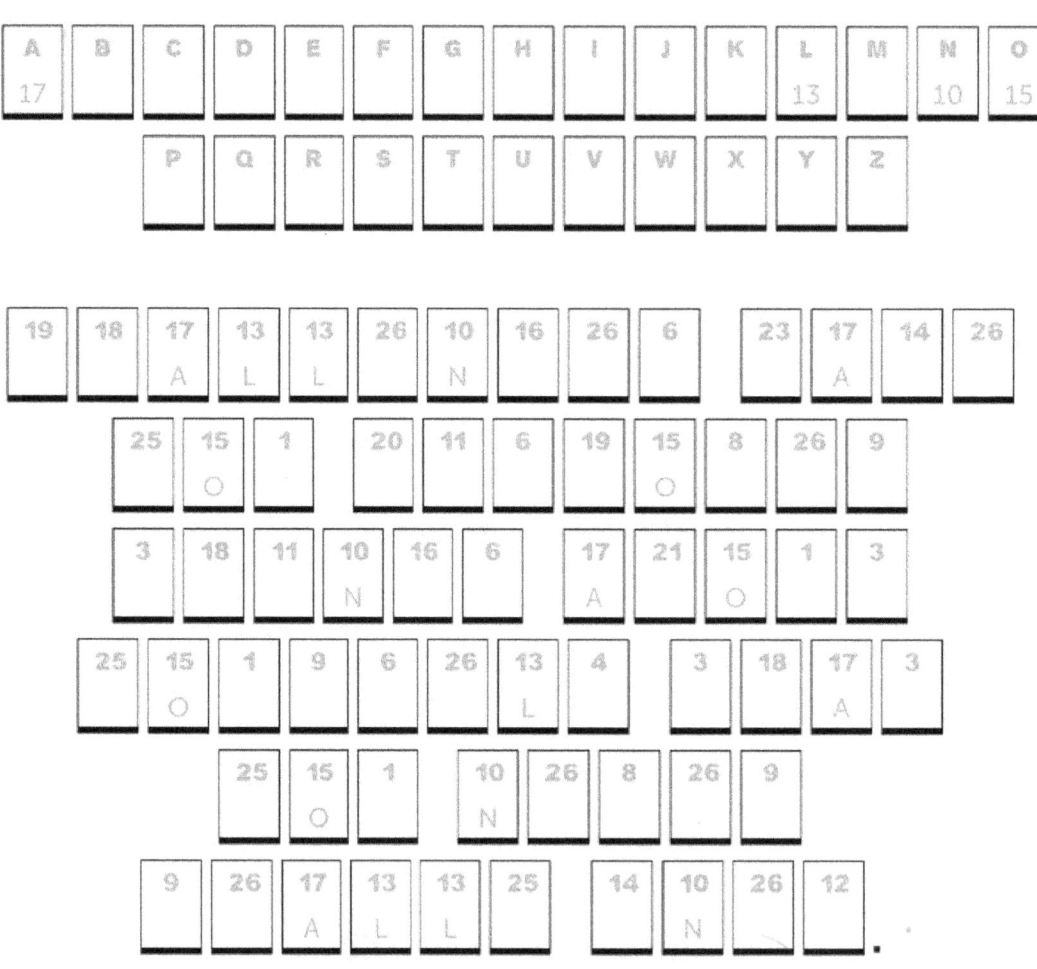

James Earl Jones

James Earl Jones

January 17, 1931 –PRESENT
ACTOR

LEFT BLANK ON PURPOSE

James Earl Jones

James Earl Jones

James Earl Jones

James Earl Jones

James Earl Jones

James Earl Jones

Directions: read the bio below and answer the following questions.

Hi, my name is James Earl Jones. I was born on January 17, 1931, in Arkabutla, MS. I graduated from Dickson Rural Agricultural School (which is now called Brethren High School) as the vice president of my class. I graduated with a Bachelor of Arts Degree from the University of Michigan. I enrolled in the Reserve Officer Training Corps program and received my commission as an Army Ranger in 1953 at the end of the Korean War. I was honorably discharged from the Army as a First Lieutenant. I began my acting career at the Ramsdell Theatre in Michigan. In 1953, I was a stage carpenter. During the 1955-1957 seasons, I was an actor and stage manager. I gave my first portrayal of Shakespeare's Othello in this theater in 1955. I won a Tony Award for my boxer role in Howard Sackler's play "The Great White Hope" and I acted in the film version. I became the second African American actor to ever receive an Academy Award nomination for their work in a movie.

1. What was the name of the college I graduate from?
    A. University of Mississippi
    B. University of Michigan
    C. University of Maryland
2. What year did I become an Army Ranger?
    A. 1953
    B. 1955
    C. 1957
3. I won a Tony Award for what?
    A. The movie The Great White Hope
    B. The play The Great White Hope
    C. The radio version of The Great White Hope

Directions: Find the words associated with James's life and career.

```
Q O C T H E S A N D L O T F W W K J
C J X I Y C W D T Y K O L C F P X Y
Q M L Z K O A U T Z U T H Y F J A T
X V F H C M P I T N F H T F W W H Z
Q T Y W U I Y Q A W B E I X Y E T J
P U K K O N L N S G C L C H L D Q A
T Z G S R G I J C X S L T I C T E R
E X I R Z 2 B A P R I O O H D L Y I
L T L A E A R I N K E N G C W Y A J
M J I W R M T E Z G K E U E B S R Q
A R T - R E V R D I K I C V N A M I
H V G R V R H R N A J I E I C W G K
U I B A W I G G G Z V R O T C A W X
Z M O T B C D M X G R H Q U R E O G
R I K S J A X W T W Z A T H Y Q B A
M I C H I G A N U N I V E R S I T Y
T Y O A D C R V E N W Z Q W A J H Y
E M L A Q J R A W N A E R O K D C F
```

Find These Words

STAR-WARS   ACTOR   COMING2AMERICA
DARTHVADER   THELIONKING   MICHIGANUNIVERSITY
HAMLET   KOREANWAR   OTHELLO
THESANDLOT

Directions: Read and answer the questions. These are your opinions so the answers will vary.

Have you ever met an entertainer in person? If so, who was it and how was it?

What is your favorite movie or TV show and who is your favorite character/actor/actress in it?

Can you name a famous entertainer who is also a writer or director?

Directions: Read and answer the questions below. There are clues in the puzzle to help you. Try and solve the cryptic message.

Clue for cryptic message: One of James's many successful films.

Questions

1) James was the first celebrity guest on ____ Street.
2) James used Darth as his handle on the CB ____ and sometimes talked like Darth Vader while using it.
3) James wasn't credited for voicing ____ Vader in the first two because he felt he was just the special effects for the character.
4) James was the first black man to play the ____ of the United States, the film was "The Man."
5) James served in the U.S. Army as a First Lieutenant in the ____.
6) James does not have an EGOT because his ____ is an honorary award.
7) James had a real bad stuttering problem until his drama classes at ____ University.

Directions: This is the WGLT Challenge. Solve the cryptogram. As the puzzle solver, you need to find which number belongs to which character. And this can be pretty challenging! You will need to match the number with the letter. There are some letters given to you below. This will help you solve the other words and unlock more characters. **Good Luck.**

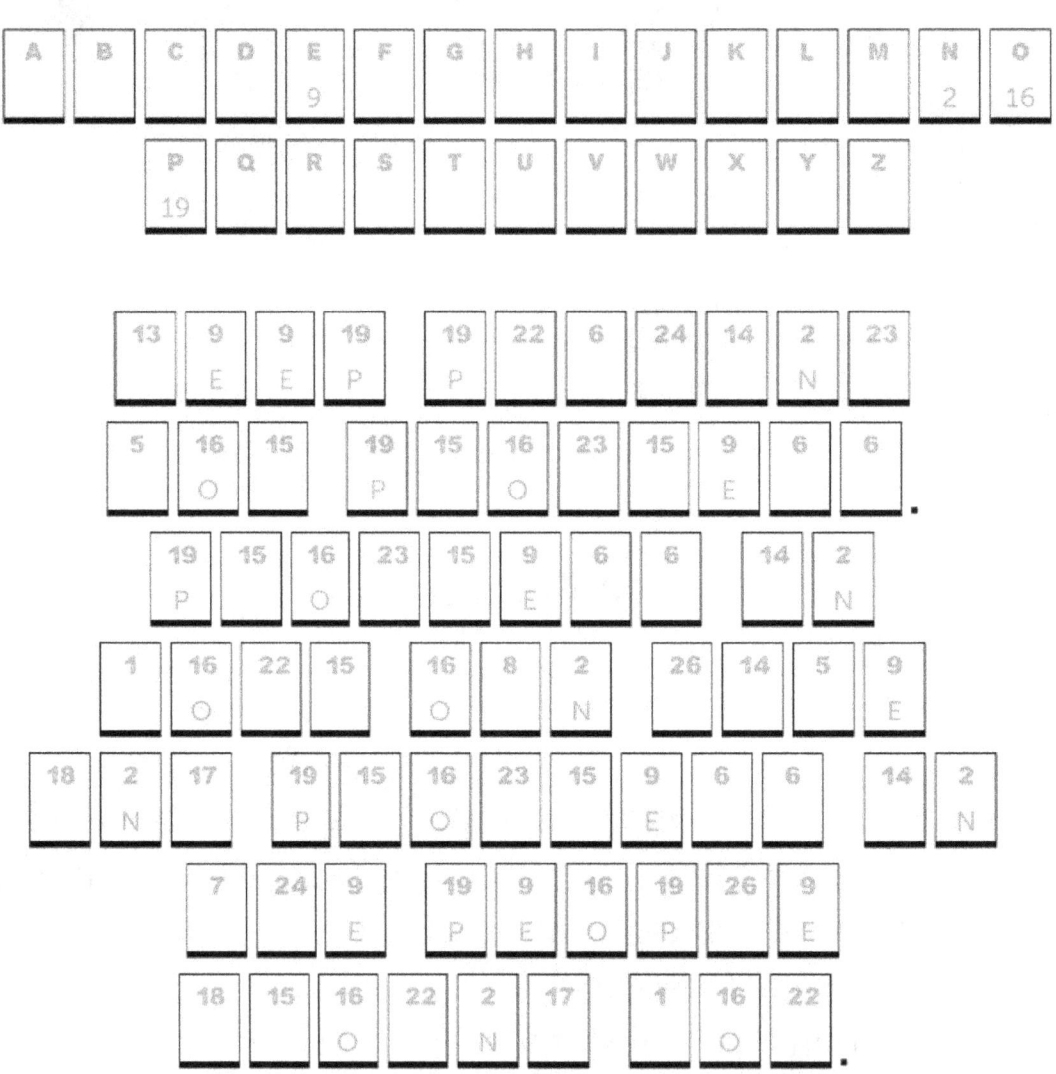

Gail Fisher

Gail Fisher

August 18, 1935 – December 2, 2000
ACTRESS   **19**

LEFT BLANK ON PURPOSE

Gail Fisher

Gail Fisher

Gail Fisher

Gail Fisher

Gail Fisher

Gail Fisher

Directions: read the bio below and answer the following questions.

Hi, my name is Gail Fisher. I was born on August 18, 1935, in Orange, NJ. I graduated from Metuchen High School. I won a few beauty pageant contests during my teenage years, such as the Miss Transit, Miss Black New Jersey and Miss Press Photographer contests. I also won a contest that was sponsored by Coca-Cola, which allowed me to spend two years studying acting at the American Academy of Dramatic Arts. I trained under Lee Strasberg and I became a member of the Repertory Theater at Lincoln Center. I was the first African American to be accepted there. I made my first television appearance in 1960 at age 25, when I appeared in the NTA Film Network program The Play of the Week. In 1970, my role on Mannix was honored when I received the Emmy Award for Outstanding Supporting Actress in a Drama Series, which made me the first African American woman to do so. In 1971, I became the first African American woman to win a Golden Globe for my role in Mannix as well.

1. Which pageant title is not one that I have won?
    A. Miss Black New Jersey
    B. Miss Press Photographer
    C. Miss Black New York
2. How old was I when I started acting?
    A. 17
    B. 22
    C. 25
3. I was the first African American woman to win?
    A. An Academy Award for Best Actress
    B. A Golden Globe Award for Best Actress
    C. A Tony for Best Actress

Directions: Answer the questions, to solve the crossword puzzle. You can use the internet if you get stuck on any question.

Across

2) Gail had a recurring guest appearance in the TV drama _____ as Judge Heller.

4) Gail landed her first _____ appearance at age 25 in the 1960 syndicated program, "Play of the Week".

5) Gail won a contest sponsored by _____, which allowed her to study acting.

6) Gail won multiple ____ awards from her performance in the TV series "Mannix."

Down

1) Gail was only the second black woman, the first being Nichelle Nichols of "Star Trek," cast as a regular _____ in a dramatic hour-long network series.

3) Gail was one of the first black actresses to appear in a ____ TV commercial with speaking lines when she did an ad for All detergent in 1961.

Directions: Read and answer the questions. These are your opinions so the answers will vary.

What do you think makes a good entertainer?

Can you name an entertainer who is also a philanthropist or activist?

Have you ever seen an entertainer perform live? If so, who was it and how was it?

Directions: Unscramble the words below about Gail. See if you can get the bonus word.

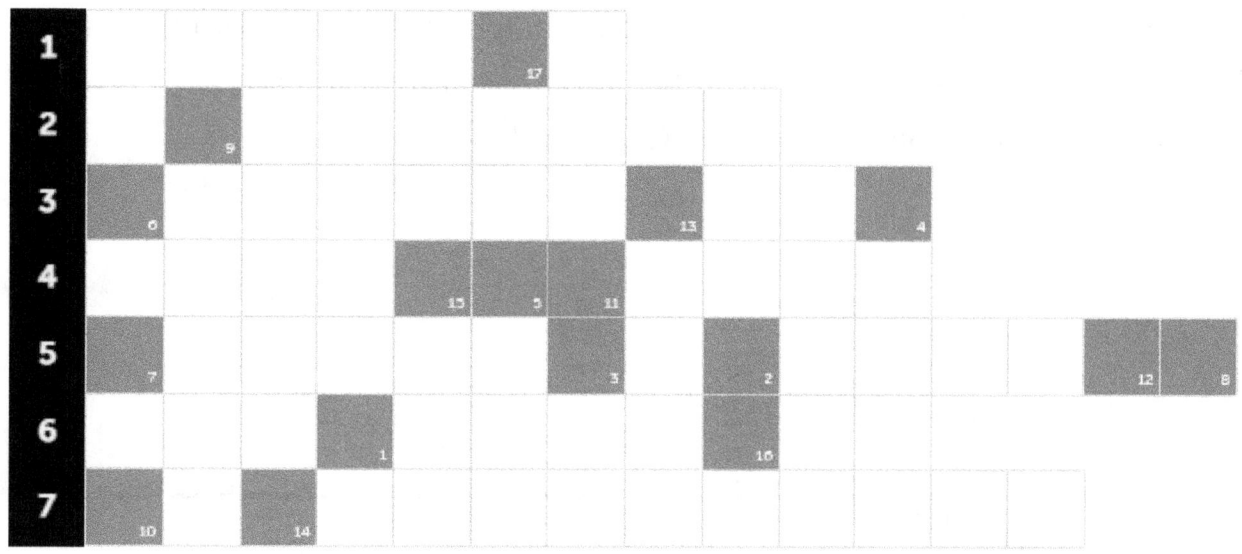

BONUS WORD

Unscramble Words

1) easrtcs
2) lo-cccoaa
3) cdaapwa-anr
4) htyenessmro
5) alrpeaghlnseito
6) rgitnhdekir
7) obeacnesttyut

Directions: This is the WGLT Challenge. Solve the cryptogram. As the puzzle solver, you need to find which number belongs to which character. And this can be pretty challenging! You will need to match the number with the letter. There are some letters given to you below. This will help you solve the other words and unlock more characters. **Good Luck.**

Sidney Poitier

Sidney Poitier

February 20, 1927 – January 6, 2022
ACTOR

Sidney Poitier

Sidney Poitier

Sidney Poitier

Sidney Poitier

Sidney Poitier

Sidney Poitier

Directions: read the bio below and answer the following questions.

Hi, my name is Sidney Poitier. I was born on February 20, 1927, in Miami, FL. I moved to New York when I was 16 to become an actor. I failed my first audition with the American Negro Theatre (ANT) because I couldn't fluently read the script. I was briefly enlisted in the Army during World War II, but I was discharged in 1944. I successfully auditioned and landed a role in an American Negro Theatre production. I filled in for Harry Belafonte in ANT production of Days of Our Youth. In 1947, I was a founding member of the Committee for the Negro in the Arts (CNA), which was an organization whose participants were committed to a left-wing analysis of class and racial exploitation. In 1955, I had my breakthrough film role as a high school student in the film Blackboard Jungle. In 1958, I played Noah Cullen in The Defiant Ones. In 1963, I played Homer Smith in Lilies of the Field and in 1964, I won the Best Actor Academy Award. I became the first African American actor to win that award.

1. **What branch of service was I enlisted in?**
   A. Navy
   B. Army
   C. Marine Corps
2. **What year did I help found the CNA?**
   A. 1948
   B. 1950
   C. 1947
3. **I was the first African American actor to do what?**
   A. Win a Golden Globe award
   B. Win an Academy Award
   C. Win an Emmy award

LEFT BLANK ON PURPOSE

Directions: Find the words associated with Sidney's life and career.

L	I	L	I	E	S	O	F	T	H	E	F	I	E	L	D	L	S
N	S	E	C	Y	I	E	B	O	L	G	N	E	D	L	O	G	T
I	A	P	N	W	K	D	Q	W	G	P	E	E	D	C	X	K	U
M	Y	A	U	Q	P	S	M	N	H	D	L	R	P	T	N	E	K
A	V	E	S	U	N	H	C	C	C	Q	C	E	A	C	I	V	J
I	R	K	E	D	M	T	K	Y	F	U	V	M	E	Z	B	C	T
M	R	F	H	O	U	B	N	Z	E	I	O	L	G	L	V	T	Z
K	A	Q	T	O	K	T	E	C	Q	L	O	X	X	F	I	Q	U
N	P	Z	N	H	F	S	R	S	P	C	H	I	C	P	Z	L	W
W	P	K	I	T	Q	C	A	I	T	X	B	D	H	P	A	S	S
F	J	B	N	H	R	G	D	V	T	A	P	X	S	C	Z	R	A
H	G	V	I	G	I	T	Q	Y	R	N	C	G	F	G	D	E	M
J	V	U	S	I	J	L	T	S	H	R	S	T	Y	U	Z	K	A
R	L	D	I	N	E	V	F	Y	K	C	J	T	O	K	E	A	H
R	L	E	A	K	H	M	C	T	A	K	F	J	U	R	V	E	A
F	W	M	R	M	J	E	S	N	X	E	X	X	N	L	H	N	B
Z	X	P	A	U	X	R	Y	A	K	I	B	J	B	Z	T	S	R
G	U	V	C	U	C	J	W	O	K	M	Q	L	V	T	H	J	W

Find These Words

BESTACTOR KNIGHTHOOD SNEAKERS
GOLDENGLOBE LILIESOFTHEFIELD DIPLOMAT
ARAISININTHESUN BAHAMAS MIAMI

Directions: Read and answer the questions. These are your opinions so the answers will vary.

What is a type of entertainment you haven't seen before but would like to try?

Who is your favorite entertainer and why?

What kind of entertainment do you enjoy most (music, movies, TV shows, etc.)?

Directions: Unscramble the words below about Cicely. See if you can get the bonus word.

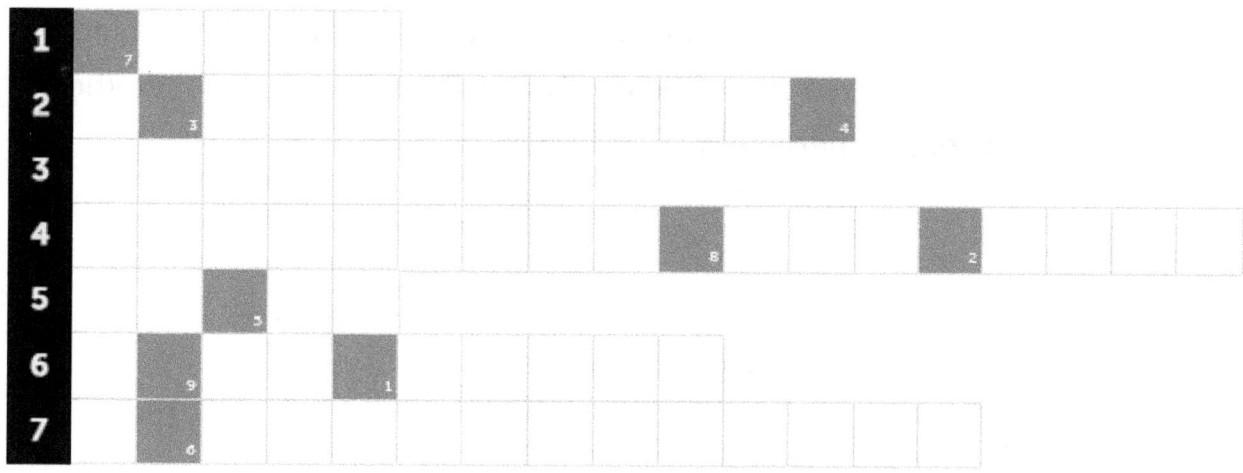

BONUS WORD

Unscramble Words

1) ocrta   **2)** trcloredimfi   **3)** hbimnaaa
4) hqnz-liea-Ilbetuee   **5)** roasc   **6)** siayaLrstt
7) bnrdtaoisemaep

Directions: This is the WGLT Challenge. Solve the cryptogram. As the puzzle solver, you need to find which number belongs to which character. And this can be pretty challenging! You will need to match the number with the letter. There are some letters given to you below. This will help you solve the other words and unlock more characters. **Good Luck.**

Phylicia Rashad

Phylicia Rashad

June 19, 1948 – PRESENT
ACTRESS 35

LEFT BLANK ON PURPOSE

Phylicia Rashad

Phylicia Rashad

Phylicia Rashad

Phylicia Rashad

Phylicia Rashad

Phylicia Rashad

Directions: read the bio below and answer the following questions.

Hi, my name is Phylicia Ayers-Allen. I was born on June 19, 1948, in Houston, TX. I graduated from Jack Yates High school. I graduated magna cum laude with a Bachelor of Fine Arts degree from Howard University. I also became a member of the Alpha Kappa Alpha sorority. I began my career by acting in Broadway plays. Some of them were Dreamgirls, The Wiz, August: Osage County, Cat on a Hot Tin Roof, Gem of the Ocean and Raisin in the Sun. In 1976, I debuted on television by acting in an episode of Delvecchio; I played Ventita Ray. In 1983, I joined the cast of the ABC soap opera One Life to Live. I played publicist Courtney Wright. From 1984–1992, I played the role of attorney Clair Huxtable on the NBC sitcom The Cosby Show. I was the first Black actress of any nationality to win the Best Actress (Play) Tony Award for my 2004 performance in the play A Raisin in the Sun. I also won the 2004 Drama Desk Award for Best Actress for the same play.

1. What is the name of my sorority?
   A. Delta Sigma Theta
   B. Zeta Phi Beta
   C. Alpha Kappa Alpha
2. What was my first TV appearance as an actress?
   A. One Life to Live
   B. Delvecchio
   C. The Cosby Show
3. I was the first black actress to win?
   A. Tony Award for Best Actress in a Play
   B. Emmy Award for Best Actress
   C. Academy Award for Best Actress

Directions: Answer the questions, to solve the crossword puzzle. You can use the internet if you get stuck on any question.

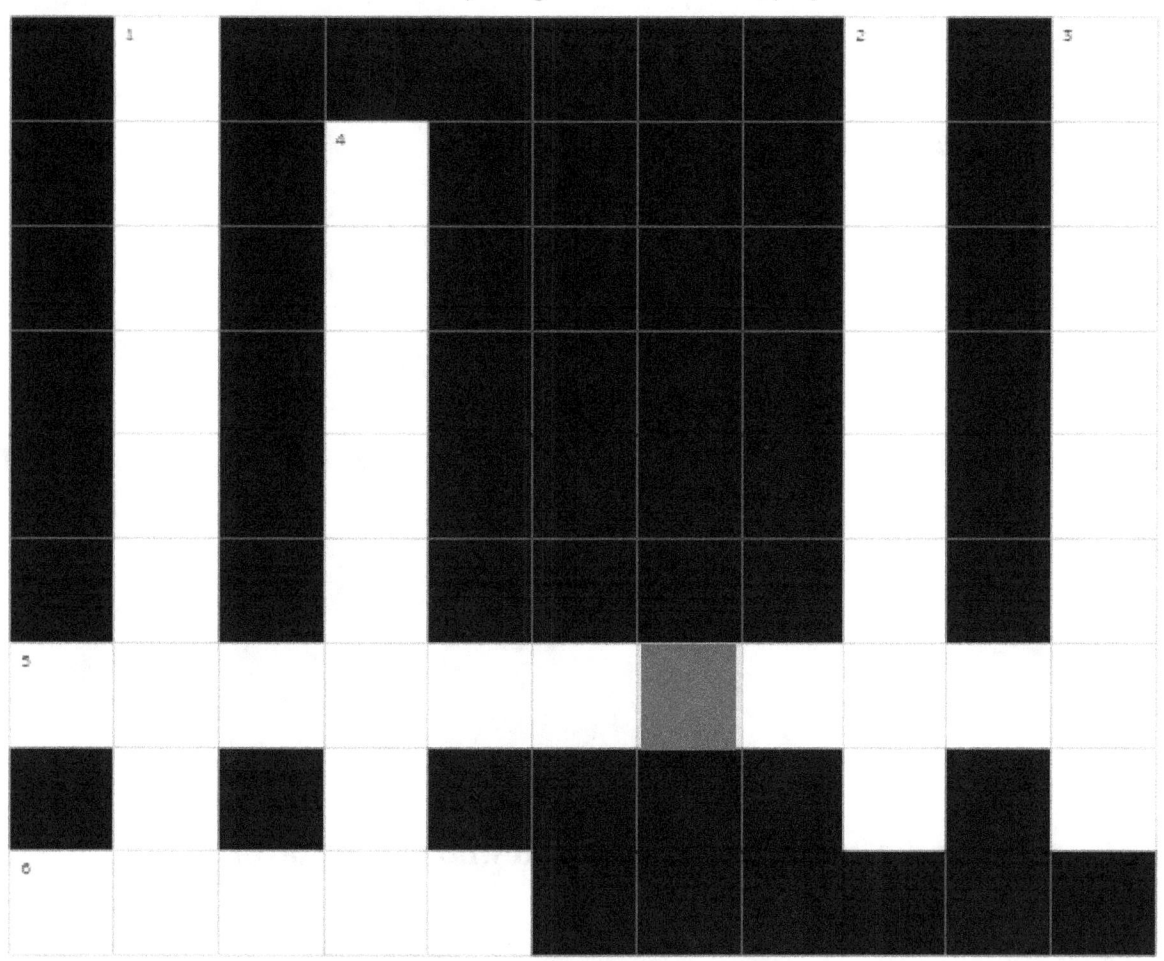

Across

5) Phylicia was the voice behind Brenda in the animated TV series '____'.

6) Phylicia tour New York city with the ____ Ensemble Company.

Down

1) Phylicia released the concept album '____ Superstar', an album that was based on Josephine Baker's life.

2) Phylicia played as a ____ in the Broadway show The Wiz.

3) Phylicia was an attorney Claire ____ in the series, The Cosby Show.

4) Phylicia stage debut as a ____ took place in 2007 with the production of 'Gem of the Ocean'.

Directions: Read and answer the questions. These are your opinions so the answers will vary.

What is your favorite movie or TV show and who is your favorite character/actor/actress in it?

_____

_____

Have you ever met an entertainer in person? If so, who was it and how was it?

_____

_____

What is your favorite movie or TV show and who is your favorite character/actor/actress in it?

_____

_____

_____

_____

_____

Directions: Unscramble the words below about Phylicia. See if you can get the bonus word.

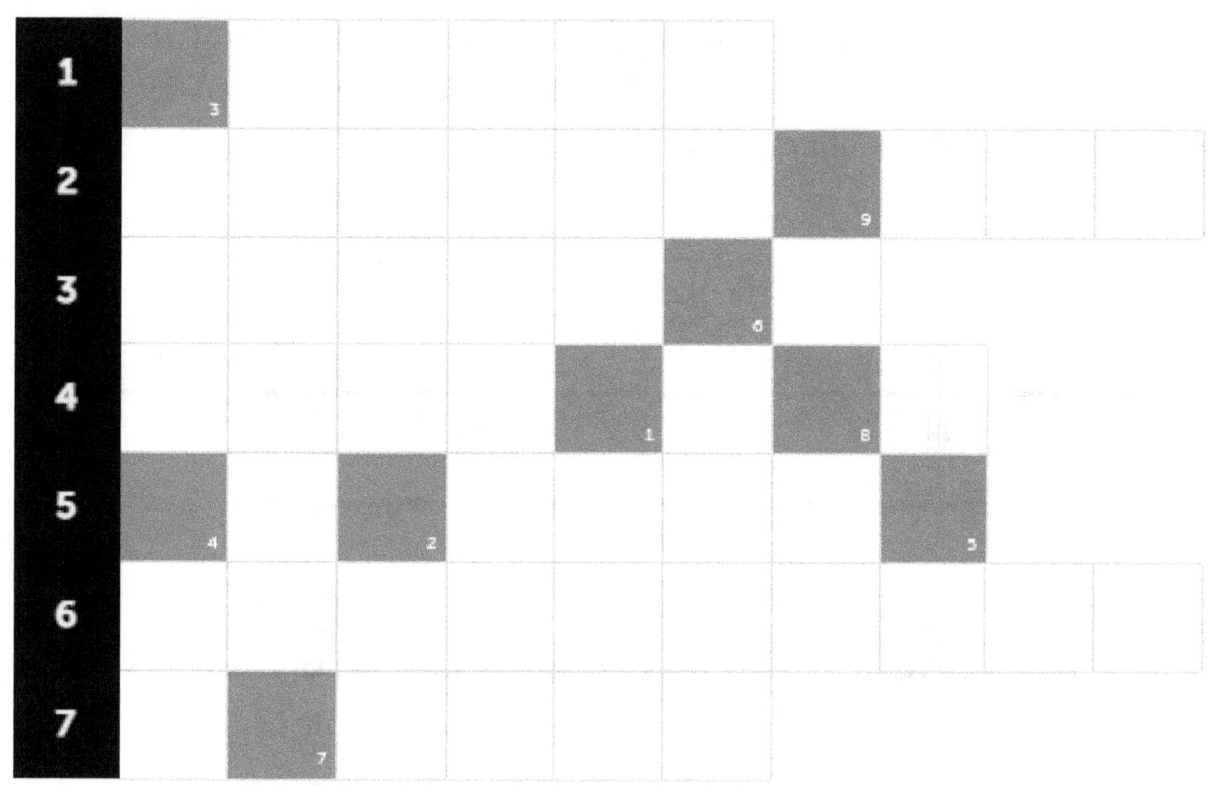

BONUS WORD

Unscramble Words

1) neirgs
2) waaapcdnra
3) sarcste
4) erdriotc
5) daoyarwb
6) ittllebill
7) wtihez

Directions: This is the WGLT Challenge. Solve the cryptogram. As the puzzle solver, you need to find which number belongs to which character. And this can be pretty challenging! You will need to match the number with the letter. There are some letters given to you below. This will help you solve the other words and unlock more characters. **Good Luck.**

A	B	C	D	E	F	G	H	I	J	K	L	M	N	O
26						4								5

P	Q	R	S	T	U	V	W	X	Y	Z
				21						

21	16	11	17	11		6	26	15	13	26	18	6
T					'		A			A		

6	5	10	11	21	16	8	22	4	21	5
	O			T				G	T	O

6	9	4	4	11	6	21	21	16	26	21
		G	G			T	T		A	T

18	5	9		15	15	22	11	1	11	17	3	11
	O		'									

13	16	5	18	5	9	13	26	22	21	11	19
		O		O			A		T		

21	5	3	11	18	5	9	17
T	O				O		

2	16	5	8	2	11	8	6	21	5
		O						T	O

21	26	12	11	8	21	5	17	12	11	11	14
T	A				T	O					

5	22	10	5	1	8	22	4
O			O				G

42

Chadwick Aaron Boseman

Chadwick Aaron Boseman

November 29, 1976 – August 28, 2020
ACTOR

LEFT BLANK ON PURPOSE

Chadwick Aaron Boseman

Chadwick Aaron Boseman

Chadwick Aaron Boseman

Chadwick Aaron Boseman

Chadwick Aaron Boseman

Chadwick Aaron Boseman

45

Directions: read the bio below and answer the following questions.

Hi, my name is Chadwick Aaron Boseman. I was born on November 29, 1976, in Anderson, SC. I graduated from T. L. Hanna High School. I received a Bachelor of Fine Arts in Directing from Howard University. I worked as the drama instructor in the Schomburg Junior Scholars Program, which was housed at the Schomburg Center for Research in Black Culture in Harlem from 2002 to 2009. I started as a playwright and stage actor in 2002 and performed in multiple productions. I won an AUDELCO Award in 2002 for my part in Ron Milner's Urban Transitions. In 2003, I was cast in my first television role in an episode of Third Watch and I began playing Reggie Montgomery in the daytime soap opera All My Children. I played some iconic roles in movies such as 42 (Jackie Robinson), Get on Up (James Brown), Marshall (Thurgood Marshall) and Black Panther (T'Challa).

1. What is the name of the HBCU that I attended?
    A. Alcorn State University
    B. Howard University
    C. Morehouse University
2. What year did I start working in Television?
    A. 2002
    B. 2004
    C. 2003
3. I played in the Marvel movie Black Panther as?
    A. M'Baku
    B. T'Challa
    C. Erik Killmonger

Directions: Find the words associated with Chadwick's life and career.

```
H A R V A R D U N I V E R S I T Y J
B G N U W K V X L Z X T Q G Q S X A
A W C M A R V E L C O M I C S S S M
I V K K I R V G F I H K Q L N V J E
N I R M R R O T C A G I P C N B R S
T R J Y V O C H Z B J R H R I D N B
H E G E F W T I K T W N M G H D R R
M H M Y Q Z F C P J D I M N U Y N O
J T B N N B R O E A N M S R H F H W
O N N K I U F O X R I R D S T M V N
O A Z H D K M S F F I R Y D D H D N
V P Q P E U G X X I O D U S P V A Z
J K S A D Q D E L M H R Y L U T E B
Y C P O V J F A O Z M A D J D I F Z
O A R L N O S N I B O R E I K C A J
U L Y T I S R E V I N U D R A W O H
S B G F N L M E Y R J X K T H R U P
A K T R S M Y V A E T Z T A H Y V C
```

Find These Words

OXFORD   DIRECTOR   HARVARDUNIVERSITY
ACTOR   BLACKPANTHER   HOWARDUNIVERSITY
MARVELCOMICS   JAMESBROWN   JACKIEROBINSON

Directions: Read and answer the questions. These are your opinions so the answers will vary.

Can you name an entertainer who is also a philanthropist or activist?

What do you think makes a good entertainer?

Can you name a famous entertainer who is also a writer or director?

Directions: Read and answer the questions below. There are clues in the puzzle to help you. Try and solve the cryptic message.

Clue for cryptic message: Chadwick went to school for this.

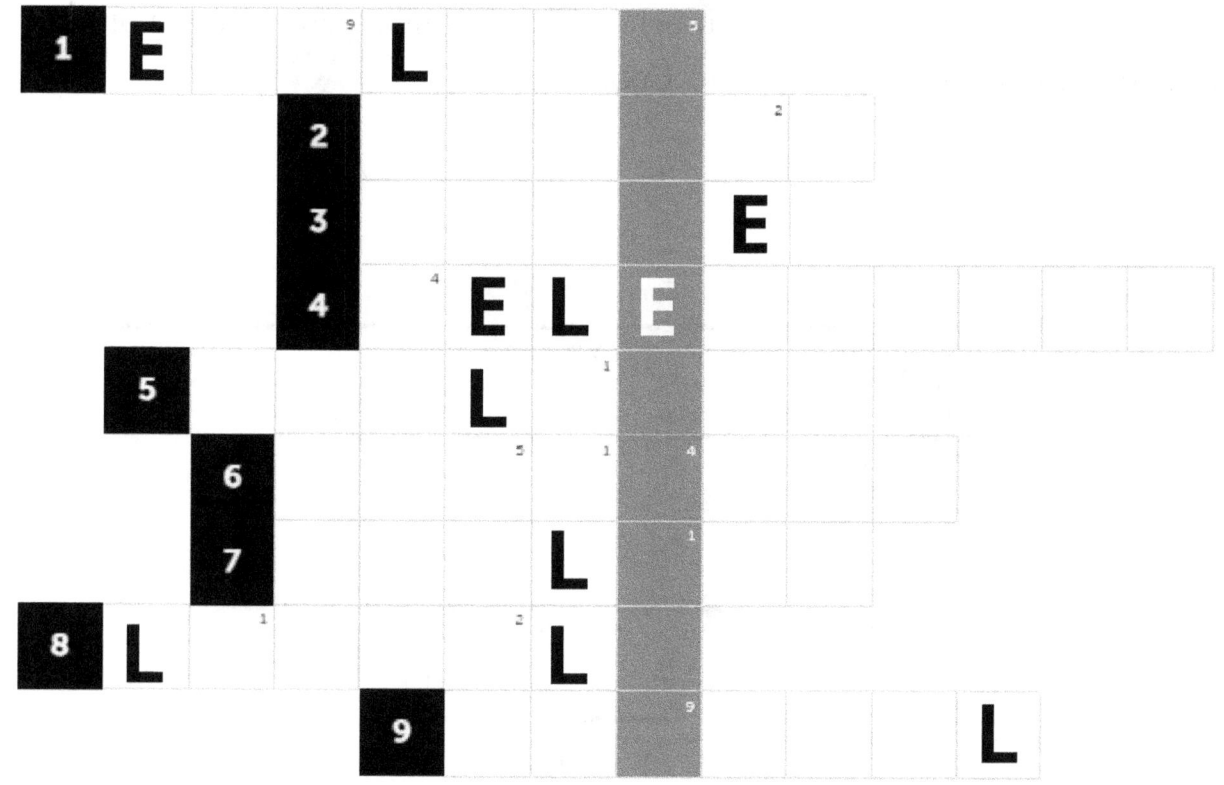

Questions

1) Chadwick studied at the British American Dramatic Academy in Oxford, ____.
2) Chadwick was a drama instructor for the Schomburg ____ Scholar's program in Harlem, NY.
3) Chadwick wrote the script for the play, Deep ____, which was performed at the Congo Square Theater Company in Chicago, IL.
4) Chadwick got his first ____ role in 2003, in an episode of Third Watch.
5) Chadwick became an Actor after taking ____ Rashad's class at Howard University.
6) Chadwick did not have to ____ for the role as Black Panther.
7) Chadwick has a Xhosa name '____'. that means 'Peacemaker'.
8) Chadwick was cast in a recurring role on the television series ____ Heights as Nathaniel Ray Taylor.
9) Chadwick graduated from New York City's ____ Film Academy.

49

Directions: This is the WGLT Challenge. Solve the cryptogram. As the puzzle solver, you need to find which number belongs to which character. And this can be pretty challenging! You will need to match the number with the letter. There are some letters given to you below. This will help you solve the other words and unlock more characters. **Good Luck.**

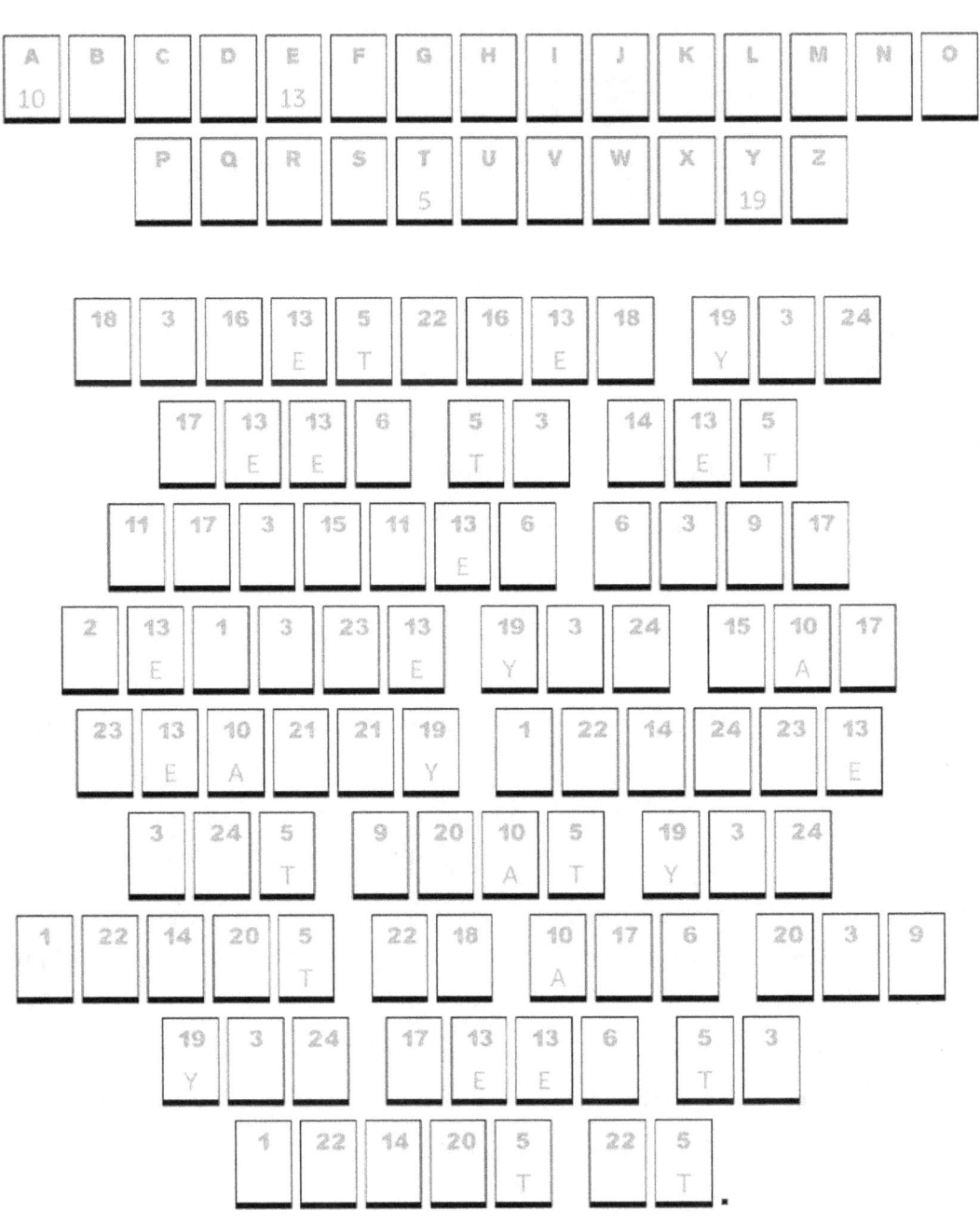

50

Oprah Winfrey

January 29, 1954 – Present
TALK SHOW HOST

51

Oprah Winfrey

Oprah Winfrey

Oprah Winfrey

Oprah Winfrey

Oprah Winfrey

Oprah Winfrey

Directions: read the bio below and answer the following questions.

Hi, my name is Oprah Winfrey. I was born on January 29, 1954, in Kosciusko, MS. At 17, I won the Miss Black Tennessee beauty pageant. I graduated from East Nashville High School. I won an oratory contest and secured a full scholarship to Tennessee State University (TSU), where I earned my bachelor's degree in speech communications and performing arts. At age 19, I was the youngest news anchor and also the first Black female news anchor at Nashville's local CBS television station. In 1976, I became a reporter and co-anchor for the ABC news affiliate in Baltimore, MD. In 1977, I became the co-host of the Baltimore morning show People Are Talking. In 1984, I host the faltering talk show AM Chicago. I turned the program into a success and in 1985, it was renamed The Oprah Winfrey Show. It was syndicated nationally in 1986 and the program became the highest-rated television talk show in the United States and earned several Emmy Awards. In 2003, I became the first Black woman billionaire in the world.

1. What is the name of the HBCU I attended?
   A. Fisk University
   B. Spellman College
   C. Tennessee State University
2. What year was The Oprah Winfrey Show started?
   A. 1985
   B. 1986
   C. 1984
3. I was the first black woman?
   A. Millionaire
   B. Billionaire
   C. Trillionaire

Directions: Answer the questions, to solve the crossword puzzle. You can use the internet if you get stuck on any question.

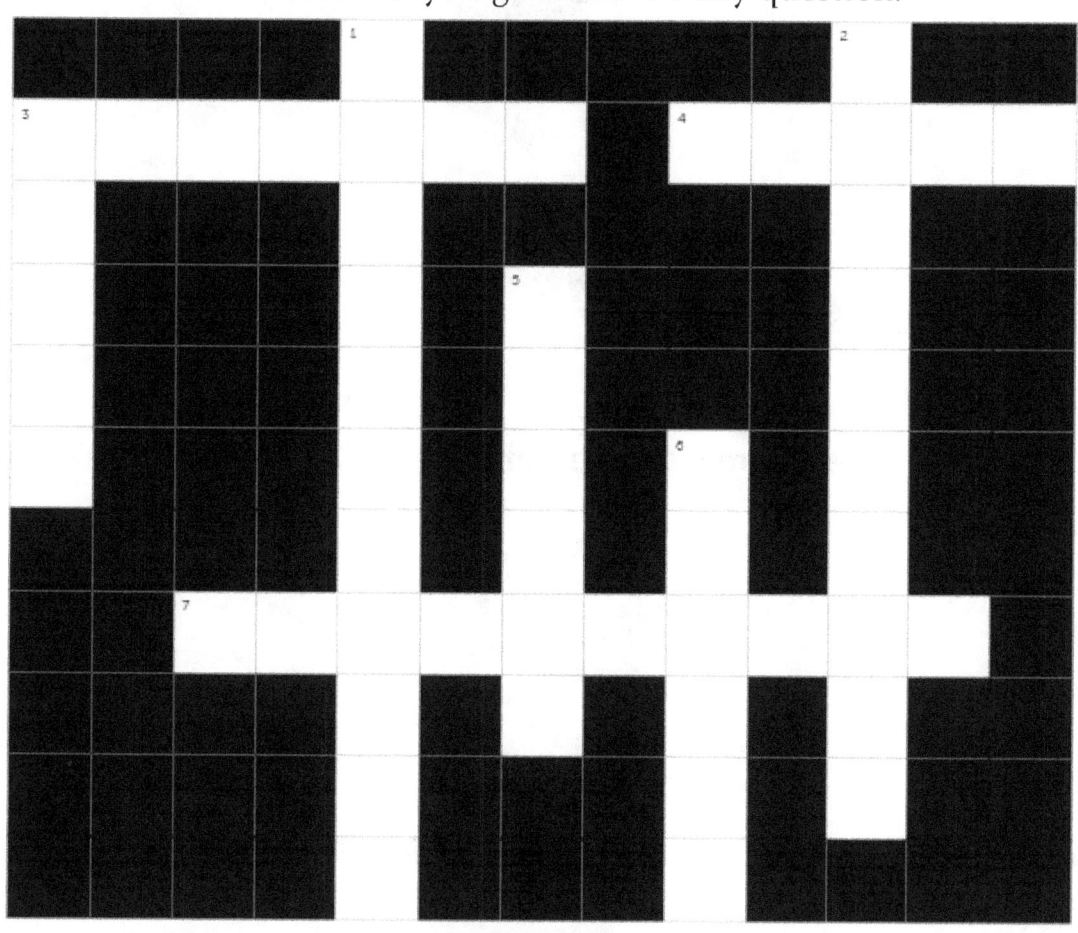

Across

3) Oprah once gave her talk show audience each a ____ car.
4) "Harpo" in Harpo Productions is ____ spelled backwards.
7) Oprah has a ____ Academy in South Africa and United States.

Down

1) Oprah is a self-made ____ with a net worth of over two billion dollars.
2) Oprah has her own ____ company called Harpo Productions. "Harpo" is Oprah spelled backwards.
3) Oprah has a ____ line with Kraft Heinz called O, That's Good.
5) Oprah helped launched ____ Media, dedicated to producing cable programming specifically for women.
6) Oprah did voice over for the cartoon character ____ the goose for Charlotte's Web.

Directions: Read and answer the questions. These are your opinions so the answers will vary.

Have you ever seen an entertainer perform live? If so, who was it and how was it?

What is a type of entertainment you haven't seen before but would like to try?

Can you name a famous entertainer from a different country?

Directions: Unscramble the words below about Oprah. See if you can get the bonus word.

BONUS WORD

Unscramble Words

1) iacoghc
2) nibarPstaOmeed
3) tasrcse
4) tuahor
5) ohoawskhstlt
6) piihspthotnral
7) oclrurpeolp
8) mlaalhfeof

Directions: This is the WGLT Challenge. Solve the cryptogram. As the puzzle solver, you need to find which number belongs to which character. And this can be pretty challenging! You will need to match the number with the letter. There are some letters given to you below. This will help you solve the other words and unlock more characters. **Good Luck.**

58

Denzel Washington

Denzel Washington

December 28, 1954 – PRESENT
ACTOR

59

LEFT BLANK ON PURPOSE

Denzel Washington

Denzel Washington

Denzel Washington

𝒟enzel 𝒲ashington

𝒟enzel 𝒲ashington

𝒟enzel 𝒲ashington

Directions: read the bio below and answer the following questions.

Hi, my name is Denzel Washington Jr. I was born on December 28, 1954, in Mount Vernon, NY. I graduated from Mainland High School. I received my Bachelor of Arts degree from Fordham University. I began to pursue acting as a career and joined the American Conservatory Theater in San Francisco. After making several successful stage performances in California and New York, I made my screen debut in 1981 in the comedy Carbon Copy. In 1982, I began to receive national attention for my work on the television drama St. Elsewhere. In 1989, I won the Oscar for Best Supporting Actor for my performance as a freed slave fighting in the Union army in the American Civil War film Glory. In 2001, I won the Academy Award for Best Actor for my role as corrupt detective Alonzo Harris in the crime thriller Training Day. Some of the other films that I'm known for are Malcolm X, Philadelphia, The Hurricane, Remember the Titans, The Great Debaters and American Gangster.

1. What college did I get my Bachelors degree from?
    A. Florida University
    B. Fordham University
    C. Texas Tech University
2. What show did I receive national attention from?
    A. St. Elsewhere
    B. Extra
    C. Mother goose a rappin' and rhymin' special
3. I won the Academy Award for Best Actor in what film?
    A. Glory
    B. Malcom X
    C. Training Day

Directions: Find the words associated with Denzel's life and career.

Z	X	R	O	T	C	E	L	L	O	C	E	N	O	B	E	H	T
Q	Z	Q	H	S	J	D	Q	L	H	R	W	C	Q	H	W	Z	J
K	P	F	O	K	M	V	C	C	T	F	E	N	C	E	S	G	C
S	T	.	E	L	S	E	W	H	E	R	E	G	P	G	W	X	S
Y	S	N	K	H	D	H	P	B	U	X	Z	B	E	I	G	A	G
B	A	I	Y	K	I	Q	C	F	G	R	S	I	S	C	J	D	M
K	E	U	X	E	X	B	G	M	A	L	C	O	L	M	X	R	U
I	X	S	S	H	G	M	K	J	X	X	F	X	E	E	I	W	G
O	W	K	T	G	J	Y	T	S	L	V	K	J	Y	W	O	J	P
N	E	L	O	A	F	N	Y	A	W	U	P	Z	E	V	B	Q	Y
F	J	U	S	A	C	G	O	L	P	R	O	D	U	C	E	R	P
J	U	B	X	B	C	T	A	T	V	W	U	U	A	S	Q	O	M
F	F	R	D	F	G	T	O	R	G	L	O	R	Y	I	V	U	V
L	G	N	E	I	O	D	O	R	W	F	H	R	Z	W	Q	S	O
S	H	A	L	V	F	Q	I	R	C	S	L	F	A	X	T	Y	N
P	I	Y	W	O	G	D	I	R	E	C	T	O	R	G	X	R	Q
F	O	R	D	H	A	M	U	N	I	V	E	R	S	I	T	Y	A
X	Z	S	U	Y	S	E	U	C	N	J	K	Y	P	N	A	U	W

Find These Words

DIRECTOR   MALCOLMX   ACTOR
PRODUCER   BESTACTOR   FENCES
ST.ELSEWHERE   GLORY   THEBONECOLLECTOR
FORDHAMUNIVERSITY

Directions: Read and answer the questions. These are your opinions so the answers will vary.

What is your favorite song and who is it by?

Can you name a famous musician who also acts?

Have you ever seen a play or musical? If so, which one and did you like it?

Directions: Read and answer the questions below. There are clues in the puzzle to help you. Try and solve the cryptic message.

Clue for cryptic message: One of Denzel's many films.

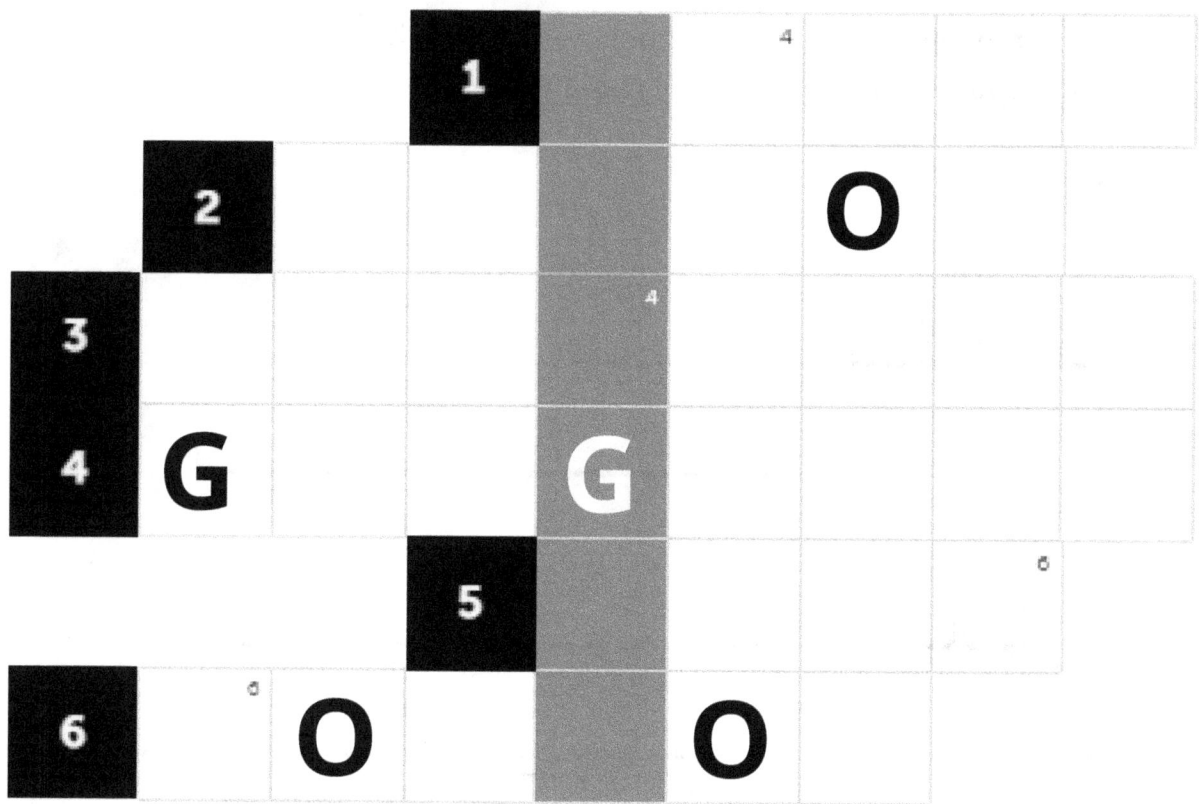

Questions

1) Denzel has been known to do most of his own stunts in his ___.

2) Denzel has the most Academy Award nominations out of his ___ black actors.

3) Denzel was sent to Oakland ___ Boarding School for his lack of discipline.

4) Denzel played drug kingpin Frank Lucas in the film American ___.

5) Denzel wrote a book called A ___ To Guide Me.

6) Denzel initially went to college to become a ___.

Directions: This is the WGLT Challenge. Solve the cryptogram. As the puzzle solver, you need to find which number belongs to which character. And this can be pretty challenging! You will need to match the number with the letter. There are some letters given to you below. This will help you solve the other words and unlock more characters. **Good Luck.**

Hattie McDaniel

Hattie McDaniel

June 10, 1893 – October 26, 1952
ACTRESS

67

LEFT BLANK ON PURPOSE

Hattie McDaniel

Hattie McDaniel

Hattie McDaniel

Hattie McDaniel

Hattie McDaniel

Hattie McDaniel

Directions: read the bio below and answer the following questions.

Hi, my name is Hattie McDaniel. I was born on June 10, 1893, in Wichita, KS. I attended Denver East High School at the same time I started professionally singing, dancing and performing skits in shows as part of The Mighty Minstrels. I dropped out of school to focus on my career. In 1914, my sister Etta Goff and I launched the McDaniel Sisters Company, which was an all-female minstrel show. I recorded and toured until the stock market crashed in 1929. I moved to Los Angeles in 1931 with my brother Sam and sisters Etta and Orlena. My brother got me a spot on the KNX radio program as Hi-Hat Hattie. In 1932, I made my first film appearance as a maid in The Golden West. In 1935, I appeared in The Little Colonel with Shirley Temple, Bill "Bojangles" Robinson and Lionel Barrymore. In 1939, I starred in Gone with the Wind as Mammy. I won the Academy Award for Best Supporting Actress for that film. I became the first African American to win an Oscar.

1. What was my stage name on the radio?
    A. Mammy
    B. Hi-Hat Hattie
    C. Queenie
2. What year did I start working in films?
    A. 1935
    B. 1939
    C. 1932
3. I became the first African American to win?
    A. Oscar
    B. Emmy
    C. Golden Globe

Directions: Answer the questions, to solve the crossword puzzle. You can use the internet if you get stuck on any question.

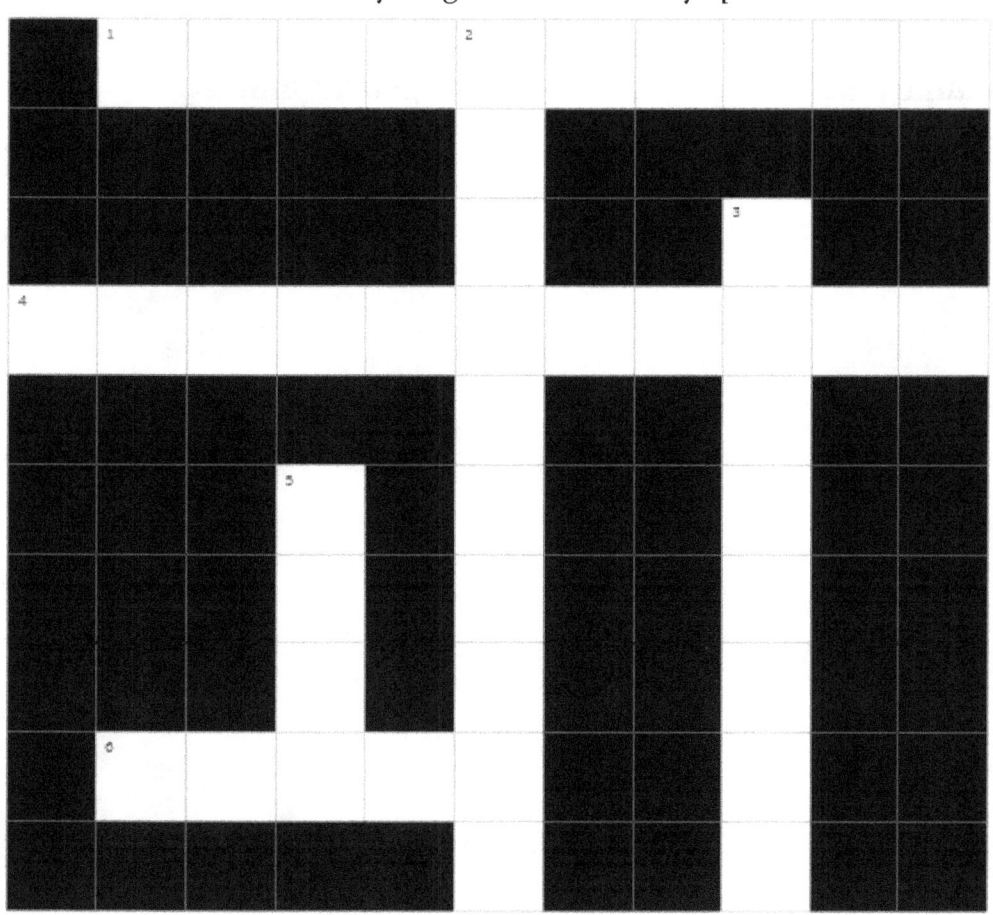

Across

1) Hattie fought to stay in areas where she lived to abide by the 14th ____, she took some to court and won.

4) Hattie honed her ____ skills while working with her brother Otis McDaniel's carnival company, a minstrel show.

6) Hattie was the first ever African American woman to ever sing on the ___.

Down

2) Hattie headlined at Sam Pick's Suburban Inn for two years before it was forced to close during the ____.

3) Hattie traveled the country as part of the chorus in the Florenz ____ touring company of Show Boat.

5) Hattie was not allowed to attend her film "Gone with the ____" premiere in deeply segregated Atlanta, GA.

Directions: Read and answer the questions. These are your opinions so the answers will vary.

Can you name a famous comedian who also acts in movies?

What is your favorite TV show and who is your favorite character/actor/actress in it?

Can you name a famous actor who also directs movies?

Directions: Unscramble the words below about Hattie. See if you can get the bonus word.

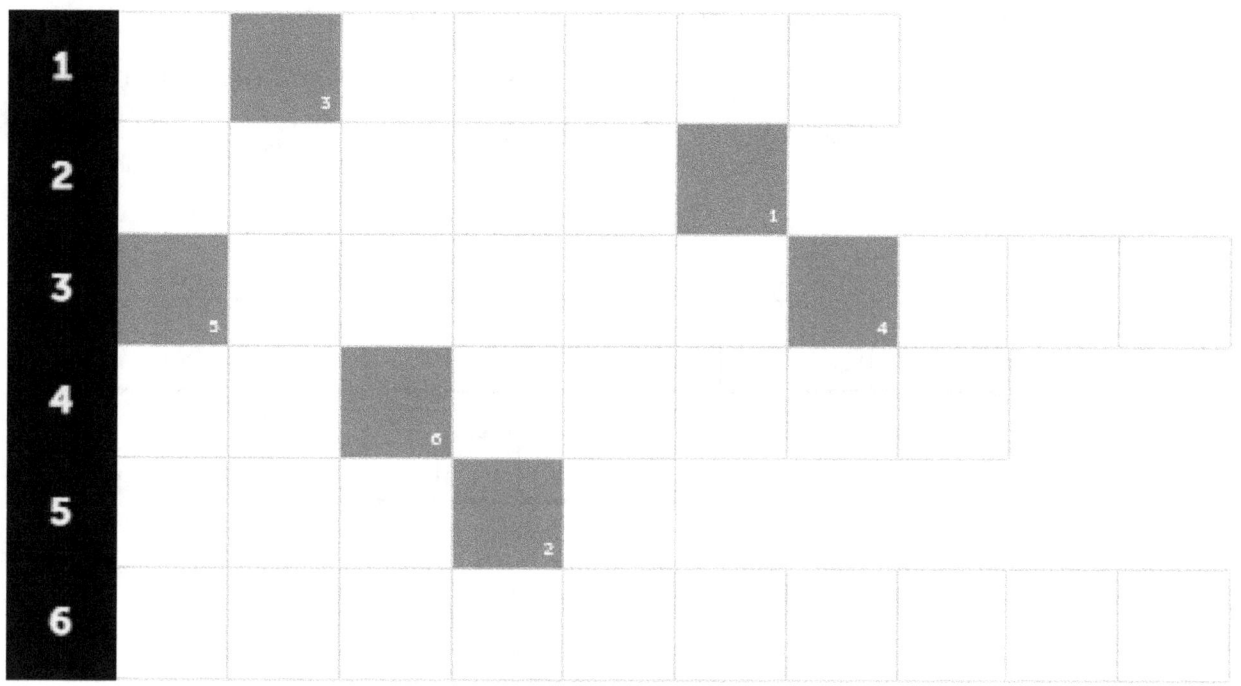

BONUS WORD

Unscramble Words

1) raetscs   **2)** ignser   **3)** rwogrisnet
4) amicoend   **5)** sraco   **6)** fmloehlafa

Directions: This is the WGLT Challenge. Solve the cryptogram. As the puzzle solver, you need to find which number belongs to which character. And this can be pretty challenging! You will need to match the number with the letter. There are some letters given to you below. This will help you solve the other words and unlock more characters. **Good Luck.**

74

Shelton Jackson Lee

Shelton Jackson Lee

July 15, 1824 – July 22, 1914
CHEF

LEFT BLANK ON PURPOSE

Shelton Jackson Lee

Shelton Jackson Lee

Shelton Jackson Lee

Shelton Jackson Lee

Shelton Jackson Lee

Shelton Jackson Lee

Directions: read the bio below and answer the following questions.

Hi, my name is Shelton Jackson Lee. I was born on March 20, 1957, in Atlanta, GA. I graduated from John Dewey High School. I took film courses at Clark Atlanta University. I received my bachelor's degree in mass communication from Morehouse College. I got my Master of Fine Arts in film and television from New York University's Tisch School of the Arts. In 1983, I premiered my first independent short film, which was titled Joe's Bed-Stuy Barbershop: We Cut Heads. This film won me a Student Academy Award. In 1986, I acted in my first feature film, She's Gotta Have It. In 1988, I made a musical called School Daze. This was a film about color discrimination (treating people differently based on their race, gender, or nationality) within the African American community. In 1989, I made the film Do the Right Thing, which showcased the biggest truth of all in our country at the time. Some other films that I have made are Jungle Fever, Malcolm X, He Got Game, Bamboozled, Chi-Raq, BlacKkKlansman and Da 5 Bloods.

1. What was the name of the HBCU that I graduated from?
    A. Clark University
    B. Morehouse College
    C. Fisk University
2. What year did I debut my first major film?
    A. 1988
    B. 1989
    C. 1986
3. Which film is not one of mine?
    A. Ghostwriter
    B. Malcolm X
    C. BlacKkKlansman

Directions: Find the words associated with Spike's life and career.

```
Z A N N A M S N A L K K K C A L B P
N E W Y O R K U N I V E R S I T Y L
F I L M D I R E C T O R S N E B G L
G O L X Q D F V U Q K J H N G I T J
N G F Z W N D R U R Y I V P E T M U
I T I F P U R E C U D O R P L S X N
H U O O 2 K R O A R R M S X L H S G
T M E X H 5 U E N Y X X H V O V B L
T Z S S U S T E T D J S D Z C C T E
H Z Q I E K J H B I X D R T E L B F
G M B E Z U V Q - R R A U J S C G E
I F S H K W T U O H E W I Q U X M V
R K Y M E H M U T I O A N N O G Y E
E D B M M Z N Q E U C U E E H M Y R
H J L A U F M X G T V O R A E C V Y
T N F L Y P F D O S G W R N R R R U
O E L L T C M R B X R Y K I O I C O
D N A M P T G A G E E N Q P M G J S
```

Find These Words

25TH-HOUR MOREHOUSECOLLEGE
PRODUCER ACTOR
NEWYORKUNIVERSITY SCREENWRITER
FILMDIRECTOR JUNGLEFEVER
BLACKKKLANSMAN DOTHERIGHTTHING

Directions: Read and answer the questions. These are your opinions so the answers will vary.

Have you ever attended a celebrity meet-and-greet or autograph session? If so, who did you meet?

What do you think is the most challenging part of being an entertainer?

Can you name a famous entertainer who is also an author?

Directions: Read and answer the questions below. There are clues in the puzzle to help you. Try and solve the cryptic message.

Clue for cryptic message: One of Spike's many films.

Questions

1) Spike's thesis film, Joe's Bed-Stuy Barbershop: We Cut Heads won a student _____ Award.

2) Spike's production company is called 40 Acres and a Mule _____.

3) Spike is known to have small and big parts in his ___.

4) Spike won the American Black Film Festival's Time Warner _____ Award in 2004.

5) Spike taught ___ courses at Harvard University.

6) Spike has become known for movies that _____ the status quo and confront the racism that's inherent within American society.

7) Spike has directed commercials for Taco Bell and Ben & _____ ice cream.

8) Michael Cimino's intense 1978 Vietnam War drama The Deer _____ inspired Spike to want to make movies.

Directions: This is the WGLT Challenge. Solve the cryptogram. As the puzzle solver, you need to find which number belongs to which character. And this can be pretty challenging! You will need to match the number with the letter. There are some letters given to you below. This will help you solve the other words and unlock more characters. **Good Luck.**

August 14, 1966 – PRESENT
ACTRESS

LEFT BLANK ON PURPOSE

Halle Berry

Halle Berry

Halle Berry

Halle Berry

Halle Berry

Halle Berry

Directions: read the bio below and answer the following questions.

Hi, my name is Maria Halle Berry. I was born on August 14, 1966, in Cleveland, OH. I graduated from Bedford High School. I won Miss Teen All American in1985 and Miss Ohio USA in 1986. In 1986, I was the first African American Miss World entrant. In 1989, I started acting in an ABC television series Living Dolls, in which I played Emily Franklin. I made my film debut in 1991 as Vivian in Spike Lee's Jungle Fever. I also had roles in Strictly Business and The Last Boy Scout. Then I played Angela in Eddie Murphy's Boomerang. In 1999, I played Dorothy Dandridge in Introducing Dorothy Dandridge. She was the first African American woman to be nominated for the Academy Award for Best Actress. A couple of years later in 2001, I played Leticia Musgrove in the film Monster's Ball. I became the first African American woman to win the Academy Award for Best Actress for my role in Monster's Ball.

1. What was the name of my first TV show appearance?
    A. The Wedding
    B. The Simpsons
    C. Living Dolls
2. What year did I start working in the film industry?
    A. 1986
    B. 1991
    C. 1989
3. I was the first African American woman to win?
    A. Academy Award for Best Actress
    B. Academy Award for Best Supporting Actress
    C. Emmy Award for Best Actress

Directions: Answer the questions, to solve the crossword puzzle. You can use the internet if you get stuck on any question.

Across

1) Halle has her own _____ company, 606 Films.
4) Halle has received a _____' Razzie award for her role in the film Catwoman.
6) Halle has a ____ edition doll for her character Jinx in the film Die Another Day.
7) Halle won and Oscar for her role in the film _____ in 2002.
8) Halle got the big-screen break in Spike Lee's film ___ Fever.

Down

2) Halle was the executive producer on Introducing ____ Dandridge in 1999.
3) Halle won many _____ pageant titles, like Miss Teen Ohio, Miss Teen America and #6 in Miss World to name a few.
5) Halle is one of the infamous Bond Girls 'Giacinta 'Jinx' ____.'

Directions: Read and answer the questions. These are your opinions so the answers will vary.

Who is your favorite voice actor and what character did they voice?

Can you name a famous entertainer who is also a dancer?

What is your favorite movie and who is your favorite character/actor/actress in it?

Directions: Unscramble the words below about Halle. See if you can get the bonus word.

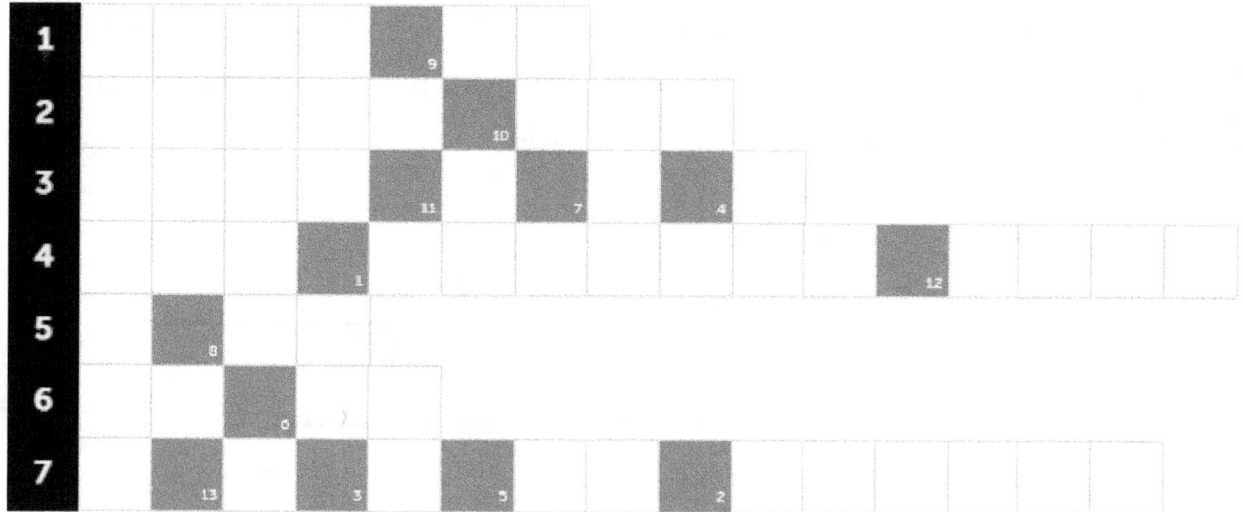

BONUS WORD

Unscramble Words

1) asrtsec
2) roabomgen
3) odaulaltsc
4) daewagroeldlobgn
5) iooh
6) mtosr
7) ctoaptnbdeeieyi

Directions: This is the WGLT Challenge. Solve the cryptogram. As the puzzle solver, you need to find which number belongs to which character. And this can be pretty challenging! You will need to match the number with the letter. There are some letters given to you below. This will help you solve the other words and unlock more characters. **Good Luck.**

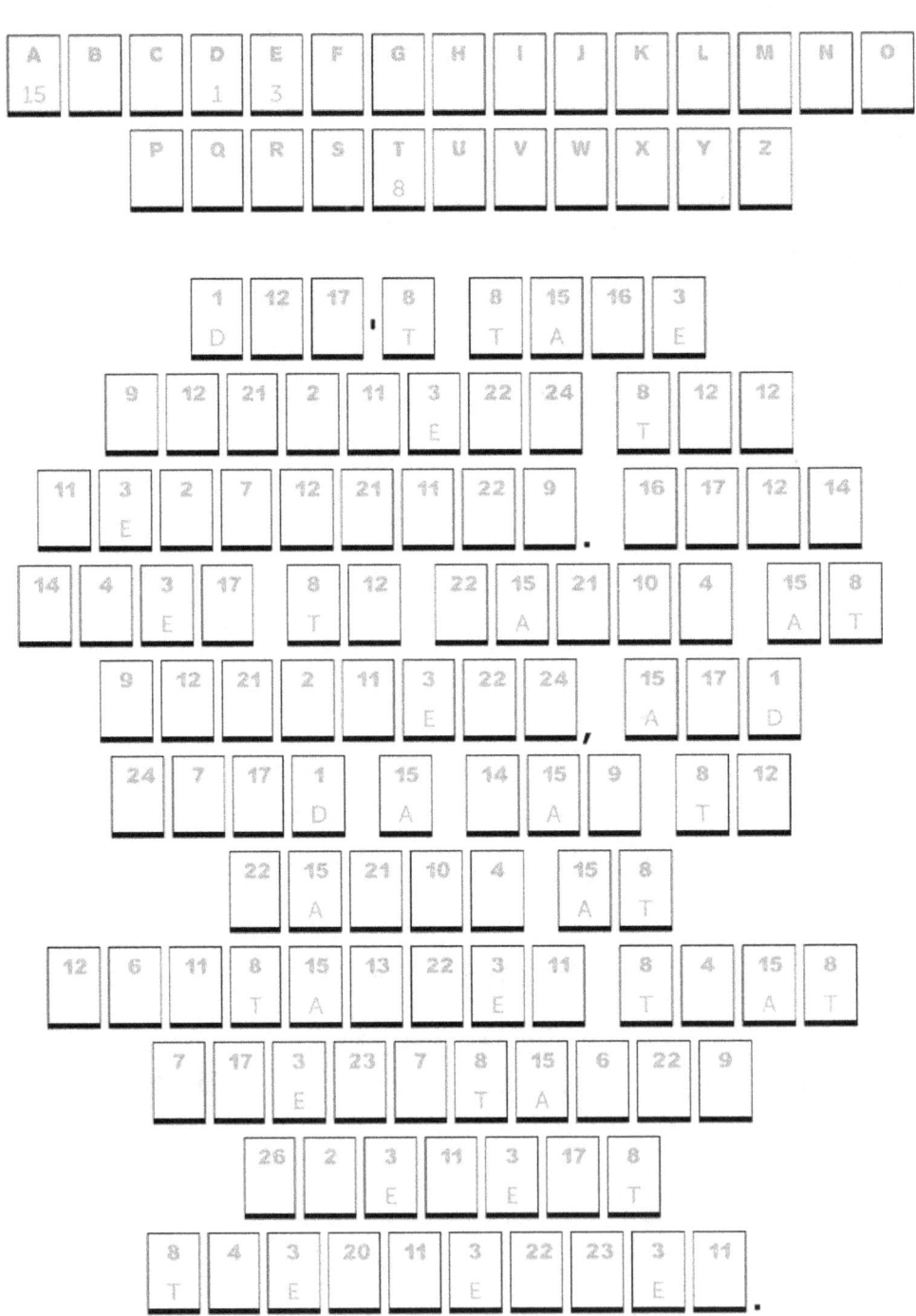

90

Tyler Perry

Tyler Perry

**September 13, 1969 –PRESENT
DIRECTOR/PRODUCER**

LEFT BLANK ON PURPOSE

Tyler Perry

Tyler Perry

Tyler Perry

Tyler Perry

Tyler Perry

Tyler Perry

Directions: read the bio below and answer the following questions.

Hi, my name is Emmitt Perry, Jr. I was born on September 13, 1969, in New Orleans, LA. I didn't graduate from high school, but I did earn my GED. In my mid-teens, I legally changed my first name to Tyler. Later on, I was watching The Oprah Winfrey Show and one of the guests described the therapeutic effect that the act of writing can have. They said that it could enable a person to work out their own problems. This inspired me to start writing a series of letters to myself, which became the basis for my first play, I Know I've Been Changed. In 1992, I financed the play with my life savings and it was a flop. Over the next few years, I rewrote it and in 1998, I performed it at the Atlanta House of Blues. It was sold out for a week straight. I used that formula to develop a large, devoted following among African American audiences. I made a series of new plays, movies and TV series, such as Diary of a Mad Black Woman, Madea's Family Reunion, Tyler Perry's House of Payne and The Haves and the Have Nots.

1. What was my birth name?
    A. Tyler
    B. Emmitt
    C. Alex
2. What year did I do my first musical?
    A. 1993
    B. 1998
    C. 1992
3. Which of these films didn't I write, direct and produce?
    A. The Have and Have Nots
    B. Madea's Family Reunion
    C. Star Trek

Directions: Find the words associated with Tyler's life and career.

```
C V V T P F P U H I X C M K V X Z Q
U E Y Y A O C A S O P V D P U X D J
B H C L W C B K G Z U I U I C P E Z
L I S E P H I T M G R I V B S V F R
K L T R A B G X Y E A W X T R P I Y
L T T P T N Q Y C G H V P A K I L X
R X R E R Q F T J O W B Y W I S M V
Y M S R O K O G E H J W C K Y G M X
R P S R L R V T O R G R Q A M N A B
X P O Y - S U Z O G F F K V X Y K O
M D R S T Y X T P R O D U C E R E O
S X C T H K C H Z S V H J O T K R B
K J X U E A B A Y C C I V N G R U F
G G E D M B L A C K P A N T H E R O
J Q L I O H O U S E O F P A Y N E K
K A A O V W P I F H G Y F Y A X D H
H O J S I X D T Q W B B K S W Y V D
G R X C E W Z K S T A R T R E K E P
```

Find These Words

BLACKPANTHER ACTOR
PAWPATROL-THEMOVIE FILMMAKER
HOUSEOFPAYNE DIRECTOR
STARTREK PRODUCER
ALEXCROSS TYLERPERRYSTUDIOS

Directions: Read and answer the questions. These are your opinions so the answers will vary.

Have you ever cosplayed as an entertainer? If so, who did you dress up as?

What do you think is the best thing about being an entertainer?

Can you name a famous entertainer who is also a visual artist (painter, sculptor, etc.)?

Directions: Read and answer the questions below. There are clues in the puzzle to help you. Try and solve the cryptic message.

Clue for cryptic message: One of Tyler's characters.

Questions

1) Tyler was inducted into the Black Music & Entertainment Walk of _____.

2) Tyler started writing because of what _____ Winfrey said during one of her shows.

3) Tyler first time _____ was in his 2006's film "Madea's Family Reunion."

4) Tyler loves listening to R & B, Jazz and _____ music.

5) Tyler first introduced audiences to his now wildly popular character Madea in his play "I Know I've Been _____."

Directions: This is the WGLT Challenge. Solve the cryptogram. As the puzzle solver, you need to find which number belongs to which character. And this can be pretty challenging! You will need to match the number with the letter. There are some letters given to you below. This will help you solve the other words and unlock more characters. **Good Luck.**

98

Lena Horne

Lena Horne

June 30, 1917 – May 9, 2010
DANCER/SINGER

LEFT BLANK ON PURPOSE

Lena Horne

Lena Horne

Lena Horne

Lena Horne

Lena Horne

Lena Horne

Directions: read the bio below and answer the following questions.

Hi, my name is Lena Horne. I was born on June 30, 1917, in Bedford-Stuyvesant, Brooklyn, NY. I attended Girls High School, but I dropped out before getting my diploma. In 1933, I joined the Cotton Club in NY. In 1935, I made my first screen appearance as a dancer in the musical short Cab Calloway's Jitterbug Party. In 1940, I went to work at the Cafe Society. In 1942, I signed with Metro-Goldwyn-Mayer(MGM). I was the first African American to be signed to a long-term studio contract (mine was for seven years). My debut film with MGM was Panama Hattie. In 1943, I performed the song "Stormy Weather" with a completely African American cast as part of Cabin in the Sky. In 1958, I became the first African American woman to be nominated for a Tony Award for Best Actress in a Musical (for my part in the "Calypso" musical Jamaica). I was the first African American person who was elected to serve on the Screen Actors Guild board of directors.

1. What was the name of the first club I joined?
    A. Cafe Society
    B. Cafe Trocadero
    C. Cotton Club
2. What film did I debut for MGM?
    A. Panama Hattie
    B. Cabin in the Sky
    C. Duchess of Idaho
3. I was the first African-American woman to?
    A. be nominated for a Academy Award for Best Actress
    B. be nominated for a Emmy Award for Best Actress
    C. be nominated for a Tony Award for Best Actress

Directions: Answer the questions, to solve the crossword puzzle. You can use the internet if you get stuck on any question.

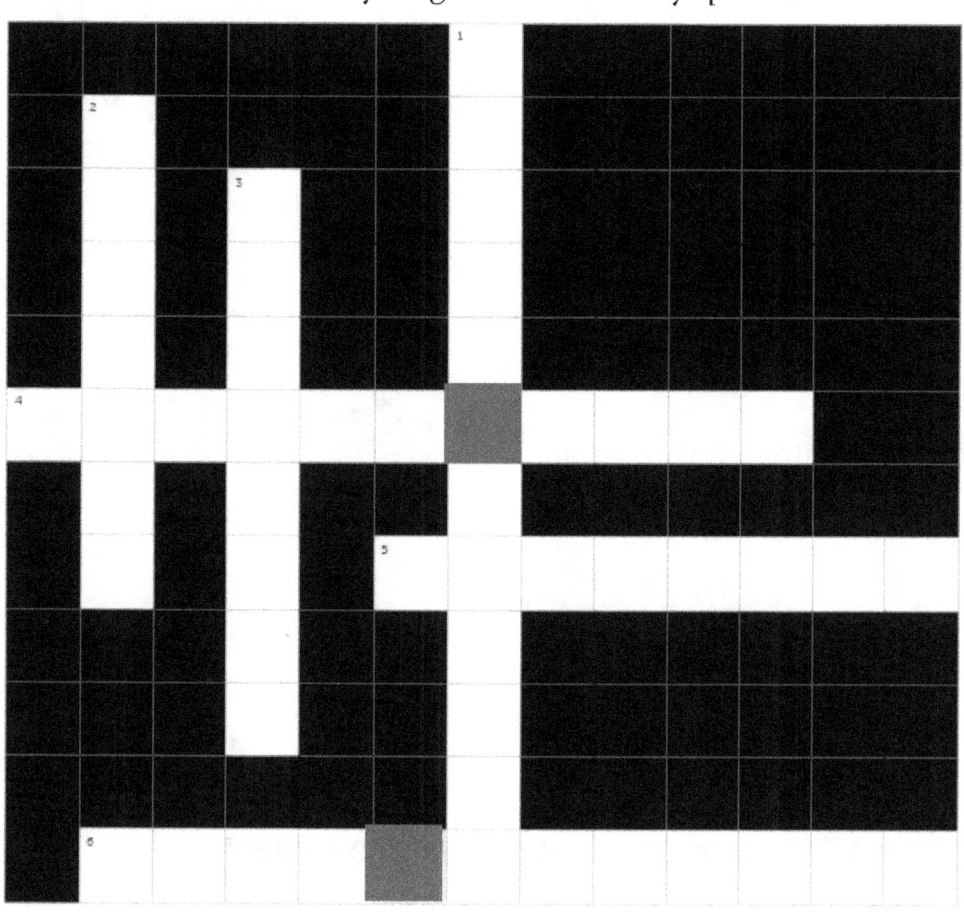

Across

4) Lena started performing at Harlem's _____ when she was 16 years old.

5) Lena was a national board member of the Progressive _____ of America, along with W.E.B. DuBois.

6) Lena performed at _____ Downtown, which was the first racially integrated club in the United States.

Down

1) Lena was a very vocal _____ advocate, refusing to perform for segregated army audiences and theaters for discrimination and working with Eleanor Roosevelt on anti-lynching legislation.

2) Lena was the second Black artist to perform at the _____ Astoria.

3) Lena appeared in many solo scenes so that her movies could be cut for _____ audiences.

Directions: Read and answer the questions. These are your opinions so the answers will vary.

Can you name a famous entertainer who is also a fashion designer?

What is your favorite genre of music?

Can you name a famous entertainer who is also a chef?

Directions: Unscramble the words below about Lena. See if you can get the bonus word.

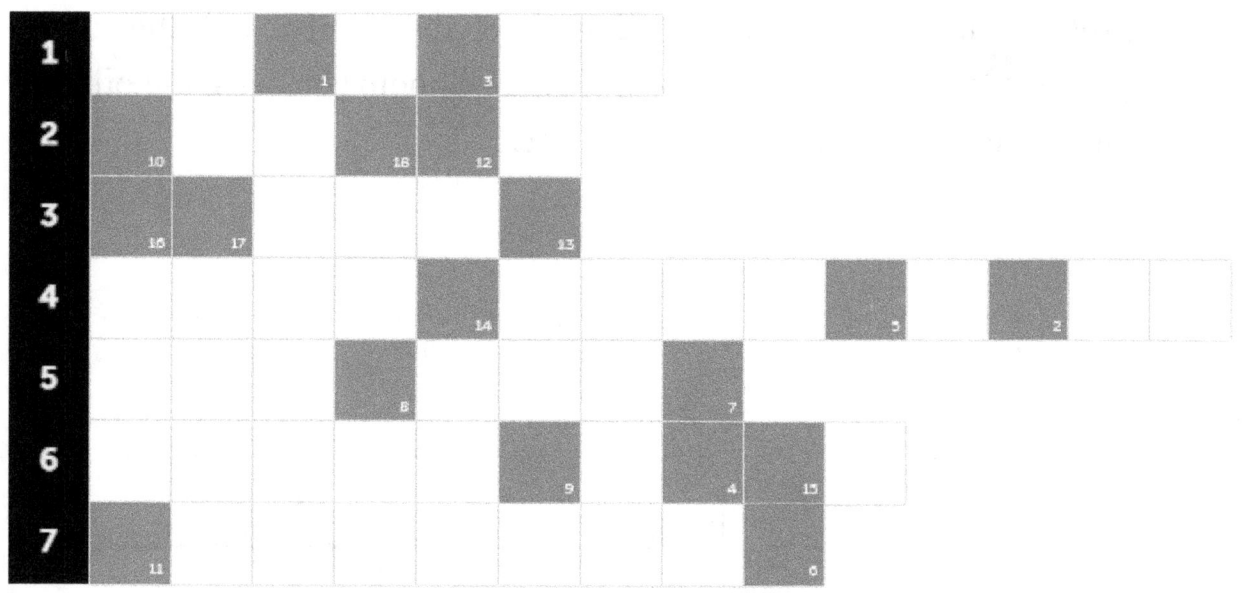

BONUS WORD

Unscramble Words

1) csrstea
2) naecrd
3) isegrn
4) htoetrwyramhes
5) odwrbaya
6) toonucclbt
7) ololdhwyo

Directions: This is the WGLT Challenge. Solve the cryptogram. As the puzzle solver, you need to find which number belongs to which character. And this can be pretty challenging! You will need to match the number with the letter. There are some letters given to you below. This will help you solve the other words and unlock more characters. **Good Luck.**

Nicholas Brothers

Nicholas Brothers

October 20, 1914 – January 24, 2006
DANCER

March 17, 1921 – July 3, 2000
DANCER

LEFT BLANK ON PURPOSE

Nicholas Brothers

Nicholas Brothers

Nicholas Brothers

Nicholas Brothers

Nicholas Brothers

Nicholas Brothers

Directions: read the bio below and answer the following questions.

Hi, my name is Fayard Antonio Nicholas. I was born on October 20, 1914, in Mobile, AL. Hi, my name is Harold Nicholas. I was born on March 27, 1921, in Winston-Salem, NC. We were fascinated by the combination of tap dancing and acrobatics. We had no formal dance training. Fayard taught himself how to dance, sing and perform by watching and imitating professional entertainers. He then taught his younger brother Harold. Harold learned by copying Fayard's moves and distinct style. We eventually became known as the Nicholas Brothers. In 1926, we gave our first performance at the Standard. In 1932, we became the featured act at Harlem's Cotton Club. We were just 11 and 18. That same year, we made our movie debut in Pie, Pie Blackbird. In 1934, we gave our first performances in a Hollywood movie, which was called Kid Millions. In 1936, we made our Broadway debut in the Ziegfeld Follies. One of our best-remembered performances is part of the movie Stormy Weather, which was released in 1943.

1. Where did we learn how to dance and sing?
    A. Dance School
    B. Singing School
    C. Self taught
2. What year did we make our Broadway debut?
    A. 1934
    B. 1932
    C. 1936
3. When we were 11 and 18 what club did we feature at?
    A. Cotton Club
    B. Standard
    C. Pearl

Directions: Find the words associated with Nicholas Brother's life and career.

B	W	W	L	M	D	Y	F	Q	X	H	E	R	L	P	D	R	W
W	N	R	Y	A	M	A	V	U	W	X	U	I	P	B	R	T	W
Y	R	A	H	T	V	Q	T	J	H	L	T	L	I	E	Y	Z	S
M	W	M	H	A	S	E	W	B	O	K	D	T	E	L	R	I	B
I	G	R	P	H	R	L	A	Z	P	S	F	Z	P	F	E	V	I
B	P	I	A	U	L	L	A	T	A	R	V	I	I	P	H	-	K
N	Y	T	B	K	G	N	E	T	G	E	T	S	E	C	T	E	O
G	X	H	P	K	K	D	S	P	N	T	M	N	B	T	A	G	S
C	G	I	O	S	U	G	V	R	D	A	R	O	L	I	E	R	X
V	W	J	I	O	Q	R	S	O	G	E	W	I	A	H	H	O	M
X	K	U	A	Z	F	P	E	N	P	B	A	L	C	I	W	E	M
H	Z	G	T	M	E	E	H	L	T	-	A	L	K	V	Y	G	M
B	H	Q	D	W	T	H	R	V	F	D	Q	I	B	L	M	-	D
X	O	Q	Z	B	D	L	J	S	R	R	V	M	I	W	R	G	W
V	T	L	F	O	B	S	G	T	C	A	H	D	R	X	O	N	H
R	W	B	U	L	C	N	O	T	T	O	C	I	D	L	T	I	B
N	X	P	W	E	A	T	L	S	B	B	C	K	V	K	S	K	V
R	D	R	J	U	M	P	I	N	J	I	V	E	D	K	B	A	N

Find These Words

HOOFERS BOARD-BEATERS COTTONCLUB
HARLEP PIEPIEBLACKBIRD KIDMILLIONS
KING-GEORGE-VI STORMYWHEATHER JUMPINJIVE

Directions: Read and answer the questions. These are your opinions so the answers will vary.

What is your favorite movie soundtrack?

_____

_____

Can you name a famous entertainer who is also an athlete?

_____

_____

What is your favorite musical artist/band and what is your favorite song by them?

_____

_____

_____

_____

Directions: Read and answer the questions below. There are clues in the puzzle to help you. Try and solve the cryptic message.

Clue for cryptic message: Nicholas Brothers performed in this city.

Questions

1) Nicholas Brothers were first the ____ Kids before there sister Dorothy left the group.

2) Nicholas Brothers were first hired for a radio program, The Horn and ____ Kiddie Hour.

3) Nicholas Brothers taught master classes in tap dance as teachers-in-residence at ____ University.

4) Nicholas Brothers was the only African Americans at that time that could interact and ____ with the all-white audience at the Cotton Club.

5) Nicholas Brothers developed a type of dance that has been dubbed "classical tap," combining jazz dance, ____ and dazzling acrobatics with tap dancing.

6) Nicholas Brothers often toured with ____ Davis Jr. throughout Europe and the United States.

Directions: This is the WGLT Challenge. Solve the cryptogram. As the puzzle solver, you need to find which number belongs to which character. And this can be pretty challenging! You will need to match the number with the letter. There are some letters given to you below. This will help you solve the other words and unlock more characters. **Good Luck.**

114

Misty Copeland

Misty Copeland

September 10, 1982 –PRESENT
BALLET DANCER

115

LEFT BLANK ON PURPOSE

Misty Copeland

Misty Copeland

Misty Copeland

Misty Copeland

Misty Copeland

Misty Copeland

Directions: read the bio below and answer the following questions.

Hi, my name is Misty Copeland. I was born on September 10, 1982, in Kansas City, MO. I graduated from San Pedro High School. I began my ballet studies at the age of 13 at the San Pedro Dance Center. When I was 14, I won a national ballet contest and I won my first solo role. In 1998, I won first place in the Los Angeles Music Center Spotlight Awards. In 2000, I joined the American Ballet Theatre (ABT) Studio Company and became a member of its corps de ballet in 2001. In 2007, I was one of the youngest dancers appointed as a soloist at the ABT. Raven Wilkinson, the first African American woman to dance for a major classical ballet company, was one of my mentors. In 2013, I danced in "Queen of the Dryads" in Don Quixote and in 2014, I performed the lead role of Swanilda in Coppélia at the Met. I was the first African American woman to dance in this role. In 2015, I became the first African American woman to be promoted to principal ballerina in ABT's 75-year history.

1. What was the name of the dance center I start at?
    A. ABT Studio Company
    B. San Pedro Dance Center
    C. San Francisco Ballet
2. I was first African American woman to dance what role?
    A. Swanilda in Coppélia at the Met.
    B. Birthday Offering at the Met
    C. Ratmansky's The Bright Stream at the Met
3. I became the first African-American woman to?
    A. be promoted to soloist in ABT
    B. be promoted to principal ballerina at NY City Ballet
    C. be promoted to principal ballerina at ABT

Directions: Answer the questions, to solve the crossword puzzle. You can use the internet if you get stuck on any question.

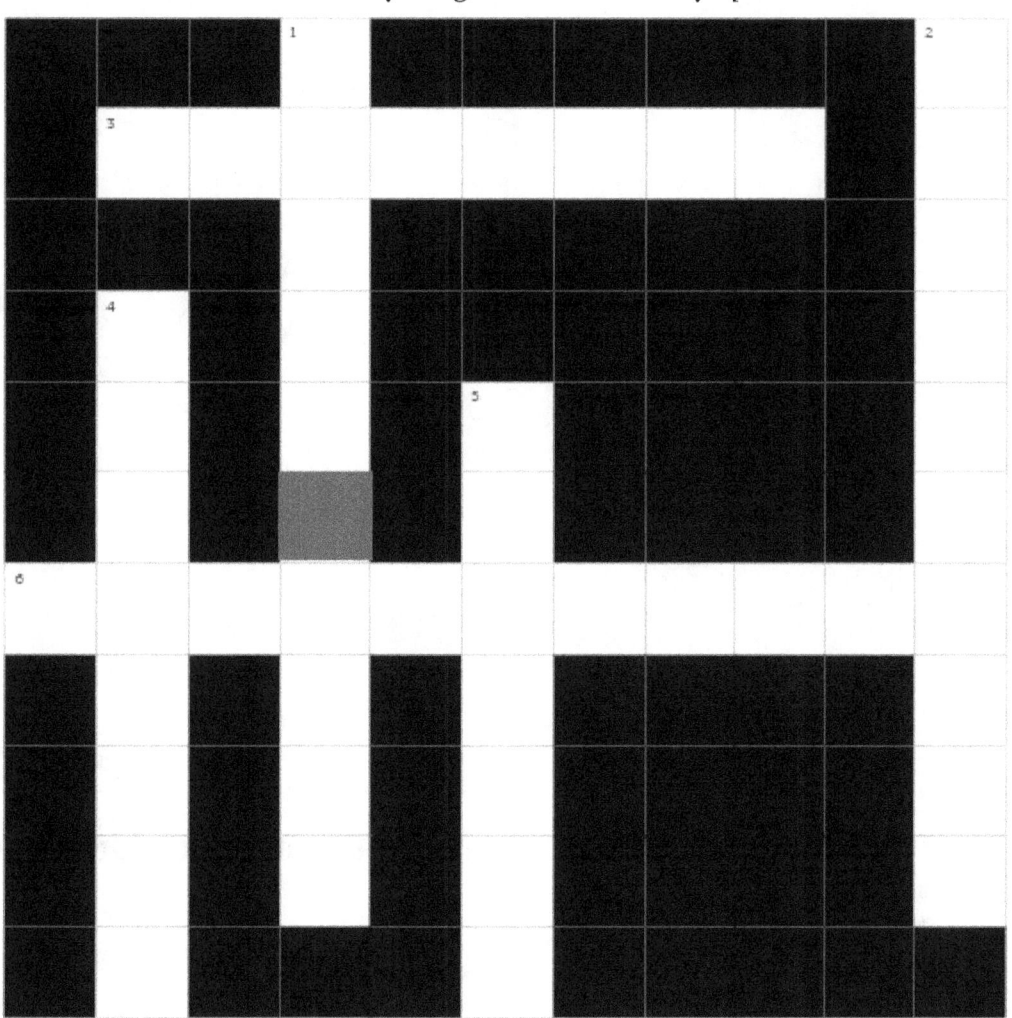

Across

3) Misty studied dance at the lauded Lauridsen Ballet Center in ____, Calif.

6) Misty faced racism after making it to the ____ ranks of the ABT, constantly being told she didn't have the body or talent for ballet.

Down

1) Misty has a book for kids, Firebird, is about a young dancer with ____.

2) Misty was awarded the Leonore Annenberg ____ in the Arts.

4) Misty didn't take her first ballet lesson until she was ____.

5) Misty appeared in a music video for Prince's version of the song "____ and Clover."

Directions: Read and answer the questions. These are your opinions so the answers will vary.

Can you name a famous entertainer who is also a photographer?

What is your favorite TV show theme song?

Can you name a famous entertainer who is also a writer of children's books?

Directions: Unscramble the words below about Misty. See if you can get the bonus word.

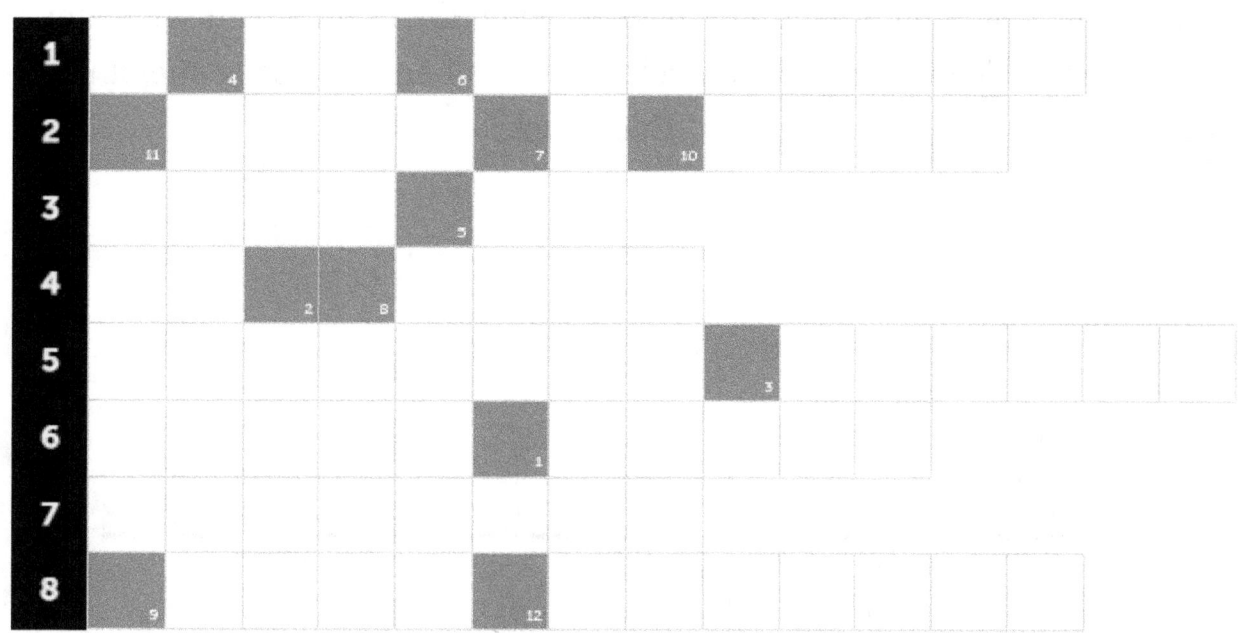

BONUS WORD

Unscramble Words

1) aedsoptclerlb
2) enltbaacdrel
3) ipgrdyo
4) badyarwo
5) aniendrcacirppl
6) asdbkezroen
7) bayoncpm
8) heucrkatrcnte

Directions: This is the WGLT Challenge. Solve the cryptogram. As the puzzle solver, you need to find which number belongs to which character. And this can be pretty challenging! You will need to match the number with the letter. There are some letters given to you below. This will help you solve the other words and unlock more characters. **Good Luck.**

Scott Joplin

Scott Joplin

November 24, 1868 – April 1, 1917
COMPOSER AND PIANIST

LEFT BLANK ON PURPOSE

Scott Joplin

Scott Joplin

Scott Joplin

Scott Joplin

Scott Joplin

Scott Joplin

Directions: read the bio below and answer the following questions.

Hi, my name is Scott Joplin. I was born on November 24, 1868, in Texarkana, TX. I attended George R. Smith College. I started playing the piano when I was 7. A man named Julius Weiss taught me throughout most of my musical education. He taught me folk, opera and classical music. He showed me that music is an art as well as entertainment. When I was 16, I started touring around towns. In 1893, I formed a band in which I played the cornet. I also arranged our band's music. When we were in Chicago for the World's Fair, my band helped with increasing the popularity of ragtime music. In 1897, I published my first ragtime song, "Original Rags". I published "Maple Leaf Rag" in 1899, which became one of the most famous ragtime pieces. I was dubbed the "King of Ragtime" by my contemporaries. Later, I signed a contract with John Stillwell Stark in 1899 for a $0.01 royalty on all sales of "Maple Leaf Rag," with a minimum sales price of 25 cents, which boosted my career and the popularity of ragtime music.

1. What was the name of the HBCU I attended?
    A. Morehouse College
    B. George R. Smith College
    C. Howard University
2. What year did I publish Maple Leaf Rag?
    A. 1898
    B. 1897
    C. 1899
3. What was my nickname?
    A. King of Ragtime
    B. King of Swing
    C. King of Jazz

Directions: Find the words associated with Scott's life and career.

```
X J A P R N S L N W N F G I O Y O P
P C O A H S I N O M E E R T B D P M
W K I E C E U G N O M U E S U M Y K
M G T O O D M N O E R P W Z M R J A
A D Z E U A K I E W A G I R U W L Y
P R W O G L N T K J G Y E I S K B X
L I K O D I E S Y X T Z D E I I T X
E F B E W A C E N T I E W U C E U O
L R W D S Q D H K R M G Y O T N A I
E E X Y F K O T P P E T U V E B M X
A H D B W S C R B I - J F N A G J K
F Z L W A N E O Q A W S S Q C O O W
R U S D V Z G J M N A R I D H M H W
A M E I T D B R X I L R W P E N Y A
G Z Q I Z C V N J S T Z C Z R T C A
O R L S M A L D Q T Z Z U O J K L C
G U R R G O W C O M P O S E R M E V
P K H C H K T A J T R U G J X W K D
```

Find These Words

PIANIST   COMPOSER   PULITZERPRIZER
MAPLELEAFRAG   TREEMONISHA   RAGTIME-WALTZ
SEDALIA   MUSICTEACHER   MUSEUM
THESTING

127

Directions: Read and answer the questions. These are your opinions so the answers will vary.

What is your favorite movie franchise and why?

Can you name a famous entertainer who is also a magician?

What is your favorite entertainer movie and who is your favorite entertainer in it?

Directions: Read and answer the questions below. There are clues in the puzzle to help you. Try and solve the cryptic message.

Clue for cryptic message: Scott's.

Questions

1) Scott wrote ____, some of his works are "A Guest of Honor" and "Treemonisha."
2) Scott wrote more than forty ___ rags.
3) Scott started his own ____ company in 1913 and started performing Treemonisha for paying audiences.
4) Scott received one penny as a ___ for his most famous work.
5) Scott published 'Maple Leaf Rag' in 1889. In the first six months, it sold around 75,000 ___.
6) Scott's music teacher was a ____ named Julius Weiss, he taught him how to play the piano.
7) Scott learned music at the early age because his ____ were musicians.

Directions: This is the WGLT Challenge. Solve the cryptogram. As the puzzle solver, you need to find which number belongs to which character. And this can be pretty challenging! You will need to match the number with the letter. There are some letters given to you below. This will help you solve the other words and unlock more characters. **Good Luck.**

Zendaya Coleman

Zendaya Coleman

September 1, 1996 – PRESENT
ACTRESS / SINGER

131

LEFT BLANK ON PURPOSE

Zendaya Coleman

Zendaya Coleman

Zendaya Coleman

Zendaya Coleman

Zendaya Coleman

Zendaya Coleman

Directions: read the bio below and answer the following questions.

Hi, my name is Zendaya Maree Stoermer Coleman. I was born on September 1, 1996, in Oakland, CA. I graduated from Oak Park High School. From an early age, I loved to perform. My interest grew from going with my mother to her job at the California Shakespeare Theater in Orinda, California. When I was young, I had several roles in productions at The Julia Morgan Theater and the American Conservatory Theater. After graduation, I started working as a fashion model for Macy's, Mervyn's and Old Navy. In 2009, I was selected to play Rocky Blue in the Disney sitcom Shake It Up (which was titled Dance Chicago at the time). In 2012, I had my first film role in Frenemies, which was a Disney Channel Original Movie. In 2012, I signed with Hollywood Records and later that year, I was one of the celebrities who competed in Season 16 of Dancing with the Stars. In 2017, I made my feature film debut as Michelle in the superhero film Spider-Man: Homecoming.

1. Which company didn't I model for?
   A. Macy's
   B. Old Navy
   C. Nordstrom
2. What is the name of my first Television show?
   A. Shake It Up
   B. Frenemies
   C. Dancing with the Stars
3. Which movie was my debut?
   A. Dune
   B. Spider-Man: Homecoming
   C. Smallfoot

Directions: Answer the questions, to solve the crossword puzzle. You can use the internet if you get stuck on any question.

Across

1) Zendaya parents are _____ and she would of been one too if not for acting.
4) Zendaya was awarded the Primetime Emmy for outstanding _____ in a drama series.
5) Zendaya the first Black woman to win the _____ for lead actress in a drama series twice.
6) Zendaya is a huge _____ fan and watches the movies a lot.

Down

2) Zendaya served as a United Nations AIDS _____.
3) Zendaya was the youngest contestant at _____ to participate in the 16th season of the show 'Dancing with the Stars'.

Directions: Read and answer the questions. These are your opinions so the answers will vary.

Can you name a famous entertainer who is also a fitness instructor?

What is your favorite TV show about animals and nature?

Can you name a famous entertainer who is also a YouTube personality?

Directions: Unscramble the words below about Zendaya. See if you can get the bonus word.

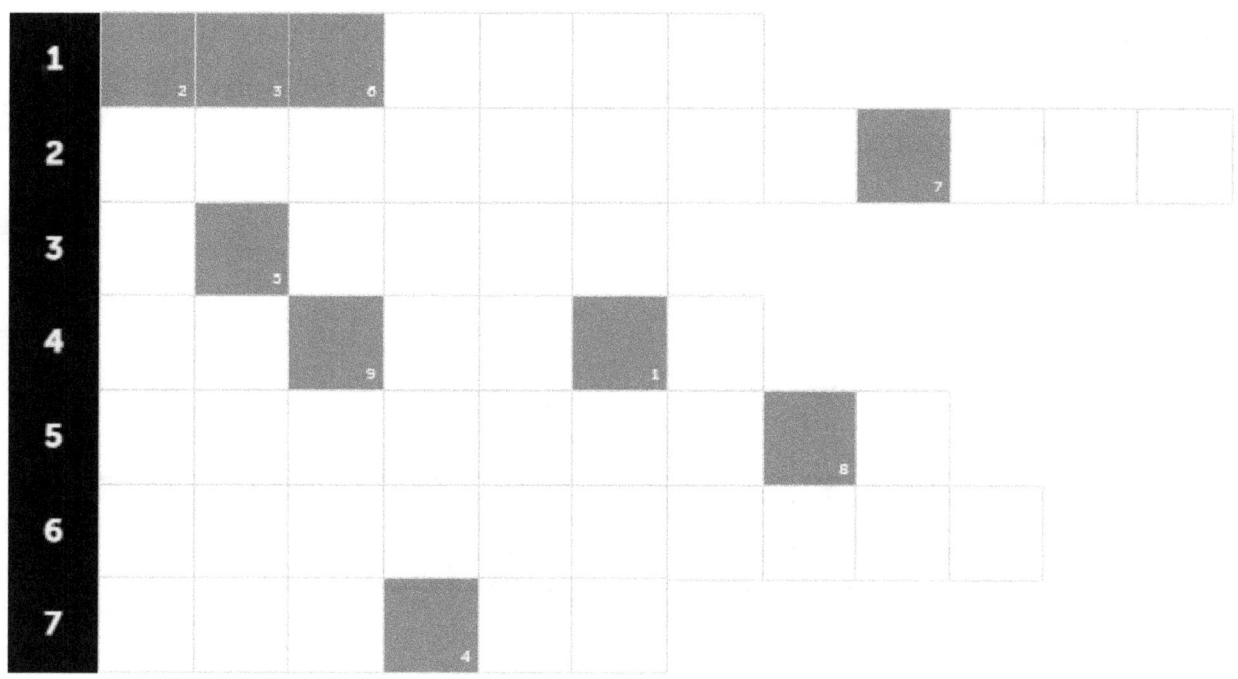

BONUS WORD

Unscramble Words

1) cewamth **2)** uvroecdercnk **3)** eysidn
4) estrcas **5)** eoybrclku **6)** naiesp-rmd
7) rneigs

137

LeVar Burton

LeVar Burton

February 16, 1957 – PRESENT
ACTOR / TELEVISION HOST

139

LEFT BLANK ON PURPOSE

LeVar Burton

LeVar Burton

LeVar Burton

LeVar Burton

LeVar Burton

LeVar Burton

Directions: read the bio below and answer the following questions.

Hi, my name is Levar Burton Jr. I was born on February 16, 1957, in Landstuhl, West Germany. I graduated from Christian Brothers High School. I got my bachelor's degree from the University of Southern California's School of Theatre. In 1976, I made my acting debut in Almos' a Man as Dave. My breakthrough role came in 1977 in the TV miniseries Roots. I played the character Kunta Kinte. In 1983, I hosted and was the executive producer of Reading Rainbow. The series lasted for 23 seasons. LeVar Burton Kids is today's version of the series. In 1986, I play the role of Lieutenant Junior Grade Geordi La Forge in Star Trek: The Next Generation. I also directed a couple of episodes of the series. In 1998, I directed The Tiger Woods Story. In 2003, I directed the film Blizzard, which stars Brenda Blethyn, Christopher Plummer, Kevin Pollak and Whoopi Goldberg. From 2017-2021, I directed NCIS: New Orleans.

1. What was the name of the college I graduated from?
    A. University of Southern California
    B. University of South Carolina
    C. University of California
2. What year did I make my acting debut ?
    A. 1977
    B. 1976
    C. 1983
3. I hosted and was the executive producer for what show?
    A. Mister Rogers' Neighborhood
    B. Jim Henson's Muppet Babies
    C. Reading Rainbow

Directions: Find the words associated with Levar's life and career.

```
D R K J M Y C M Y T E M W W Y K M
X F V P R I Z D C W O F S N C E J
J V J P R P E A B O D Y A W A R D
D M V P Z P C N B J O M B N R T A
R T M P D H R K A T R A H O K R H
T S O H N O S I V E L E T W F A L
Q F J Q J X F O G A G C O M Z T N
W J N U L C E M M Y A W A R D S E
V V S D I K N O T R U B R A V E L
D R O W N E K O P S T S E B D J X
N S U C U E T T V I H F L N O O P
L A X N V S R U O E O I Q V O N F
O N J R E A D I N G R A I N B O W
```

Find These Words

ACTOR   AUTHOR   BESTSPOKENWORD   EMMYAWARDS   GERMANY

LEVARBURTONKIDS   PEABODYAWARD   READINGRAINBOW   STARTREK

TELEVISONHOST

143

Directions: Read and answer the questions. These are your opinions so the answers will vary.

What is your favorite horror movie and why?

Who is your favorite entertainer and why?

What kind of entertainment do you enjoy most (music, movies, TV shows, etc.)?

Directions: Read and answer the questions below. There are clues in the puzzle to help you. Try and solve the cryptic message.

Clue for cryptic message: Levar's first audition.

Questions

1) LeVar's first book, ____, was published in 1997 and was named a Wordstock bestseller.

2) Sacramento renamed Meadowview Park after LeVar, dubbing it LeVar ____ Park.

3) LeVar enrolled in a ____ seminary when he was only 13 to become a Priest and studied there for four years, but decide to take a different path.

4) LeVar's breakthrough role of ____ Kinte in the seminal mini-series Roots on what was his very first professional acting audition.

5) LeVar directed the ____ Channel original movie Smart House.

Directions: This is the WGLT Challenge. Solve the cryptogram. As the puzzle solver, you need to find which number belongs to which character. And this can be pretty challenging! You will need to match the number with the letter. There are some letters given to you below. This will help you solve the other words and unlock more characters. **Good Luck.**

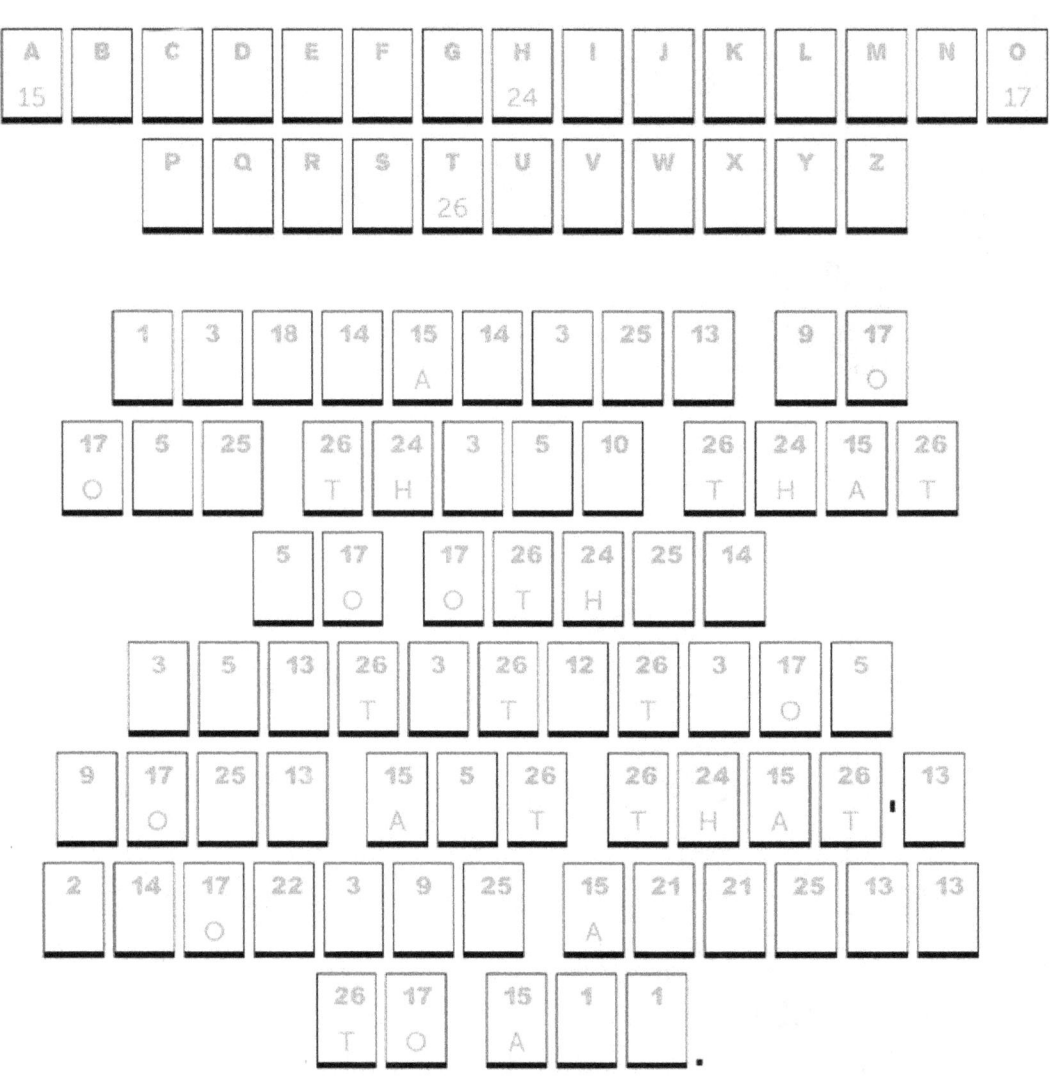

Diahann Carroll

Diahann Carroll

July 17, 1935 – October 4, 2019
ACTRESS / SINGER

LEFT BLANK ON PURPOSE

Diahann Carroll

Diahann Carroll

Diahann Carroll

Diahann Carroll

Diahann Carroll

Diahann Carroll

Directions: read the bio below and answer the following questions.

Hi, my name is Carol Diann Johnson. I was born on July 17, 1935, in the Bronx, NY. When I was 15, I modeled for Ebony magazine. I graduated from LaGuardia High School of Music and Performing Arts. I attended New York University, where I majored in sociology. When I was 18, I appeared as a contestant on the DuMont Television Network program Chance of a Lifetime. I won the top prize and I won for the next four weeks. I performed at Cafe Society and Latin Quarter nightclubs. In 1954, I made my film debut; I played a supporting role in Carmen Jones. From 1961–1962, I starred alongside Sidney Poitier in the film Paris Blues. In 1962, I became the first African American woman to win a Tony Award for Best Actress, which I received for my role in the Broadway musical No Strings. In 1968, I became the first African American actress to star in my own television series, which was called Julia. Notably, I did not play a domestic worker. I won the Golden Globe Award for Best Actress in a Television Series after the show's first year.

1. What was the name of the magazine I modeled for at 15?
    A. JET
    B. Ebony
    C. Time
2. What year did I make my film debut?
    A. 1961
    B. 1955
    C. 1954
3. I was the first African-American woman to win a?
    A. Tony Award for best actress
    B. Emmy Award for best actress
    C. Golden Globe Award for best actress

Directions: Answer the questions, to solve the crossword puzzle. You can use the internet if you get stuck on any question.

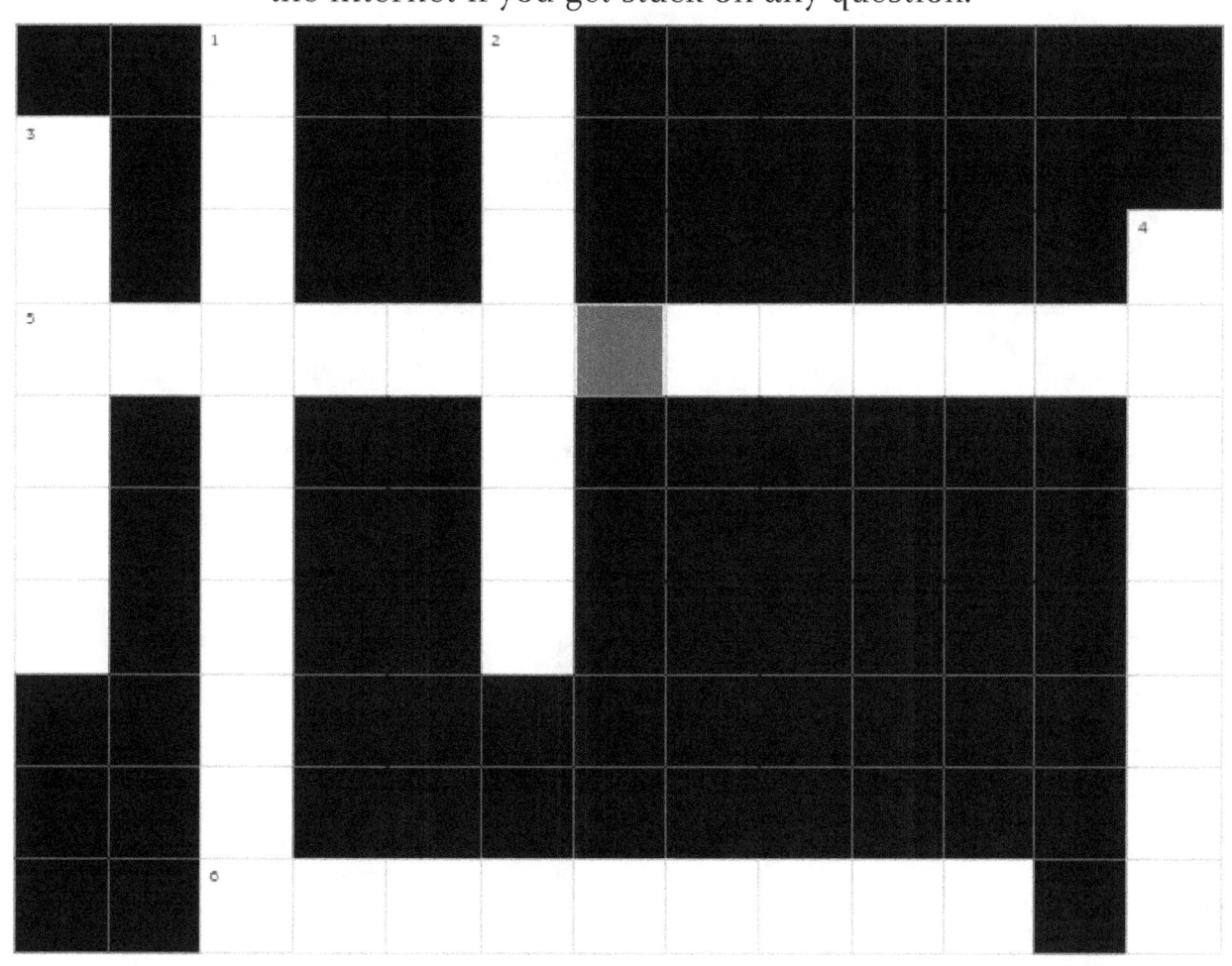

Across
5) Diahann is a _____ survivor as well as an advocate.
6) Diahann worked as a model and _____ singer as a teenager.

Down
1) Diahann starred in her own _____ series named "Julia."
2) Diahann played recurring character Jane Burke on Grey's _____.
3) Diahann began releasing _____ in the late 1950s like "Best Beat Forward" and "Showstopper!."
4) Diahann made her _____ stage debut starring in Harold Arlen and Truman Capote's "House of Flowers."

Directions: Read and answer the questions. These are your opinions so the answers will vary.

Can you name some famous entertainers from different genres (comedy, drama, action, animation, etc.)?

_____

_____

Have you ever met an entertainer in person? If so, who was it and how was it?

_____

_____

What is your favorite movie or TV show and who is your favorite character/actor/actress in it?

_____

_____

_____

_____

_____

Directions: Unscramble the words below about Diahann. See if you can get the bonus word.

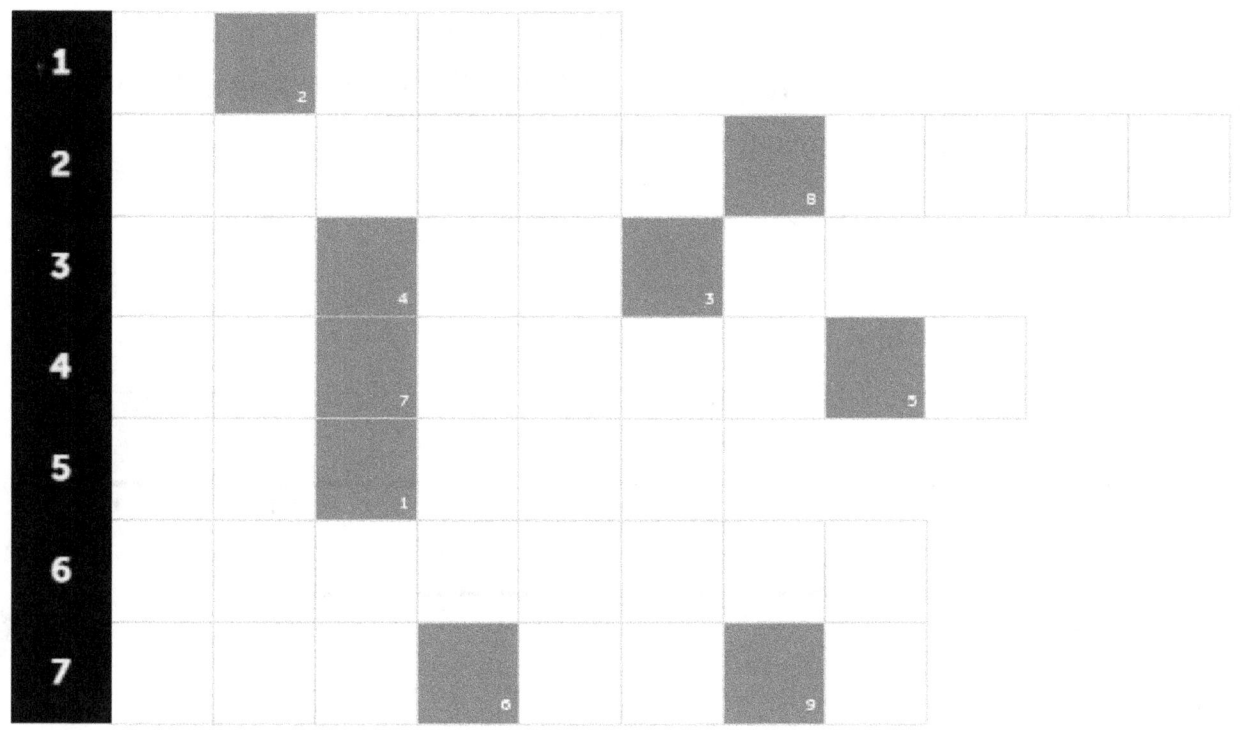

BONUS WORD

Unscramble Words

1) demlo
2) doggbloeenl
3) srtseac
4) ynawordta
5) insreg
6) eianuldc
7) cistavti

Directions: This is the WGLT Challenge. Solve the cryptogram. As the puzzle solver, you need to find which number belongs to which character. And this can be pretty challenging! You will need to match the number with the letter. There are some letters given to you below. This will help you solve the other words and unlock more characters. **Good Luck.**

Harry Belafonte

Harry Belafonte

March 1, 1927 – April 25, 2023
SINGER

LEFT BLANK ON PURPOSE

Harry Belafonte

Harry Belafonte

Harry Belafonte

Harry Belafonte

Harry Belafonte

Harry Belafonte

Directions: read the bio below and answer the following questions.

Hi, my name is Harold George Bellanfanti Jr. I was born on March 1, 1927, in Harlem, NY. I attended George Washington High School, but I dropped out to enlist in the U.S. Navy and contribute to the World War II effort. I was a member of the Navy from 1944 to 1945. In 1945, I returned to New York City. I used my GI Bill benefits to pay for my classes at The New School Dramatic Workshop, where I worked alongside my lifelong friend, Sidney Poitier. In 1949, I launched my recording career as a pop singer on the Roost label. I switched paths a few times and I debuted at The Village Vanguard, which was a legendary jazz club. In 1953, I signed a contract with RCA Victor. Later that year, I released my first widely received single, "Matilda." In 1956, I released my breakthrough album, Calypso. It became the first LP in the world "to sell over 1 million copies within a year". It was also the first million-selling album ever in England. I was dubbed the "King of Calypso." In 1959, I was the first Jamaican American to win an Emmy for Revlon Revue: Tonight, with Belafonte.

1. What branch of the military did I serve in?
    A. Marine Corps
    B. Army
    C. Navy
2. What year did I start my singing career?
    A. 1949
    B. 1953
    C. 1959
3. I was the first Jamaican American to win?
    A. Oscar
    B. Emmy
    C. Golden Globe

Directions: Find the words associated with Harry's life and career.

```
W T X Q G L F W E J H S V E A X P H
J H S F Z L G Y E U N D G U C A Q R
Y E Q I G Z M O S P Y L A C T V L O
W B I L N P L O X X P Q U X O J N D
U A C R Z G O R Q T E A Z R R W C B
R N B N E U E W L B P Q C C F A P Z
H A O B E T D R I B B B B R R M H H
A N W E T I I X Y U M T E M A L X O
V A H R A T W R I P Y N E V M S P P
U B M X N O M Q W G X N F S J N N G
I O R G I N Y L Q G J R W E W U B P
R A Q J C Y R D F O N C P U Q E R Y
C T Z U E A P J N N G O P L Z O L K
W S C M N W W E N A L Q S B N H Q G
A O Q H T A S Y U D Y M S T G A K B
H N L B K R I A T S I V I T C A A J
E G K L U D E G A N T S U C Q L L A
G H V S U D N A P G V N R R I D N X
```

Find These Words

SONGWRITER   TONYAWARD   SINGER
CARMENJONES   ACTIVIST   ACTOR
CALYPSO   THEBANANABOATSONG   BLUES

Directions: Read and answer the questions. These are your opinions so the answers will vary.

Can you name a famous entertainer who is also a writer or director?

What do you think makes a good entertainer?

Can you name an entertainer who is also a philanthropist or activist?

Directions: Read and answer the questions below. There are clues in the puzzle to help you. Try and solve the cryptic message.

Clue for cryptic message: Harry use to sing this genre.

Questions

1) Harry's parents were Jamaican and he lived with his ___ in Jamaica for eight years.
2) Harry's film debut was "Bright ____" in 1953.
3) Harry was the lead role in "____ of Our Youth" at Harlem's American Negro Theater.
4) Harry first signed with The Roost Label in 1949 and sang mostly ___ during that time.
5) Harry received the Recording Academy's ____ Achievement Award.
6) Harry enlisted into the Navy and served in ___ War II.

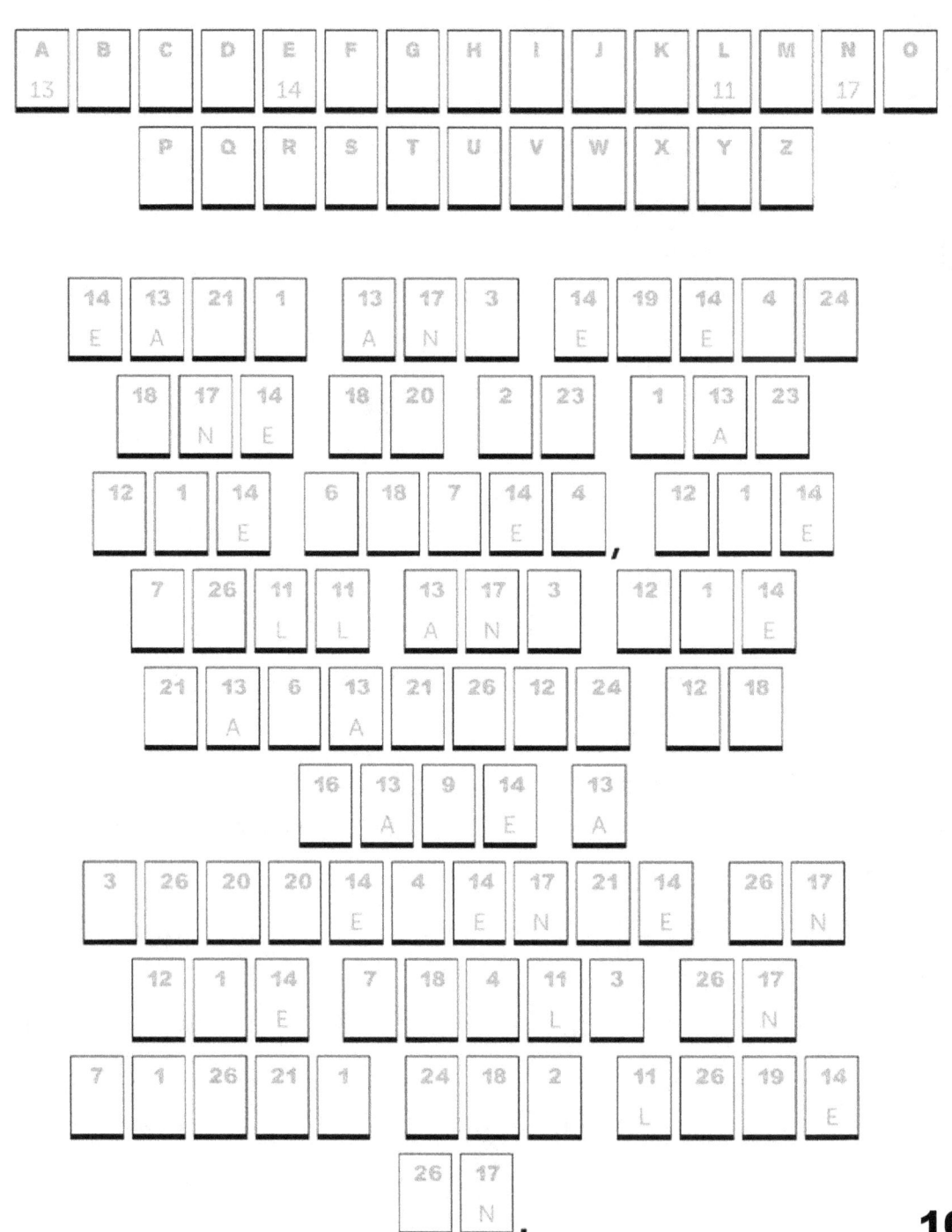

Angela Evelyn Bassett

Angela Evelyn Bassett

July 15, 1824 – July 22, 1914
CHEF

LEFT BLANK ON PURPOSE

Angela Evelyn Bassett

Angela Evelyn Bassett

Angela Evelyn Bassett

Angela Evelyn Bassett

Angela Evelyn Bassett

Angela Evelyn Bassett

Directions: read the bio below and answer the following questions.

Hi, my name is Angela Evelyn Bassett. I was born on August 16, 1958, in New York City, NY. I graduated from Boca Ciega High School. I got my bachelor's degree in African American studies and my master's in the School of Drama from Yale University. In 1985, I made my first television appearance in Doubletake. In 1986, I made my film debut as a news reporter in F/X. In 1991, I had my breakout role in the movie Boyz n the Hood. The next year, I played the role of Betty Shabazz in the film Malcolm X. In 1993, I played Tina Turner in the film What's Love Got to Do with It. In 1995, I acted in the classic film Waiting to Exhale as Bernadine "Bernie" Harris. Some of the other films and TV shows that I acted in are How Stella Got Her Groove Back, Mr. 3000, The Jacksons: An American Dream, The Rosa Parks Story, 9-1-1, Akeelah and the Bee, Meet the Robinsons, Olympus Has Fallen and Black Panther.

1. What is the name of the college I went to?
    A. Harvard University
    B. Yale University
    C. Berkeley University
2. What year did I debut in films?
    A. 1986
    B. 1985
    C. 1991
3. In Malcolm X I played the role of?
    A. Ramonda
    B. Betty Shabazz
    C. Tina Turner

Directions: Answer the questions, to solve the crossword puzzle. You can use the internet if you get stuck on any question.

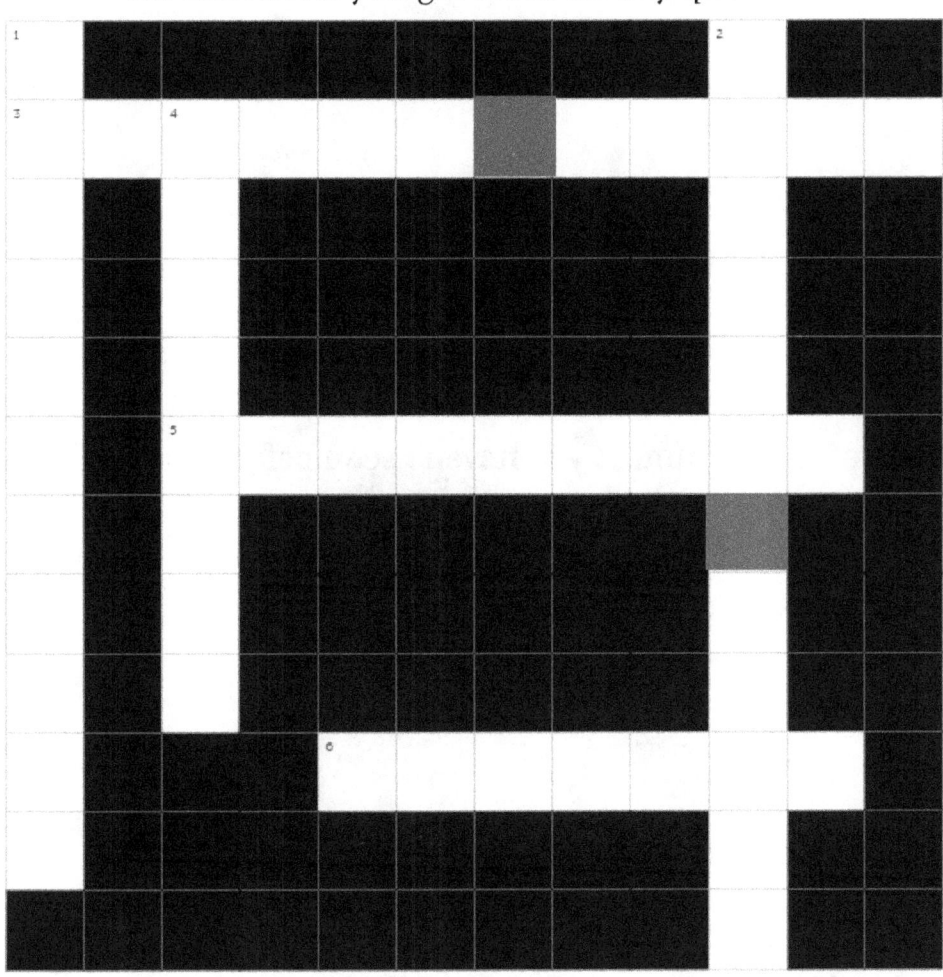

Across

3) Angela appeared in American ____: Roanoke and directed its sixth episode
5) Angela provided her voice for the 2007 film Meet the ____.
6) Angela was the narrator of the Magic ____ nighttime spectacular Disney Enchantment.

Down

1) In High School Angela was a ____ and a member of the Upward Bound college prep program, the debate team, student government, drama club and choir.
2) Angela won a ____ and earned an Academy Award nomination for her portrayal of Tina Turner.
4) Angela made her film debut as a news ____ in F/X.

Directions: Read and answer the questions. These are your opinions so the answers will vary.

Have you ever seen an entertainer perform live? If so, who was it and how was it?

What is a type of entertainment you haven't seen before but would like to try?

What is your favorite song and who is it by?

Directions: Unscramble the words below about Angela. See if you can get the bonus word.

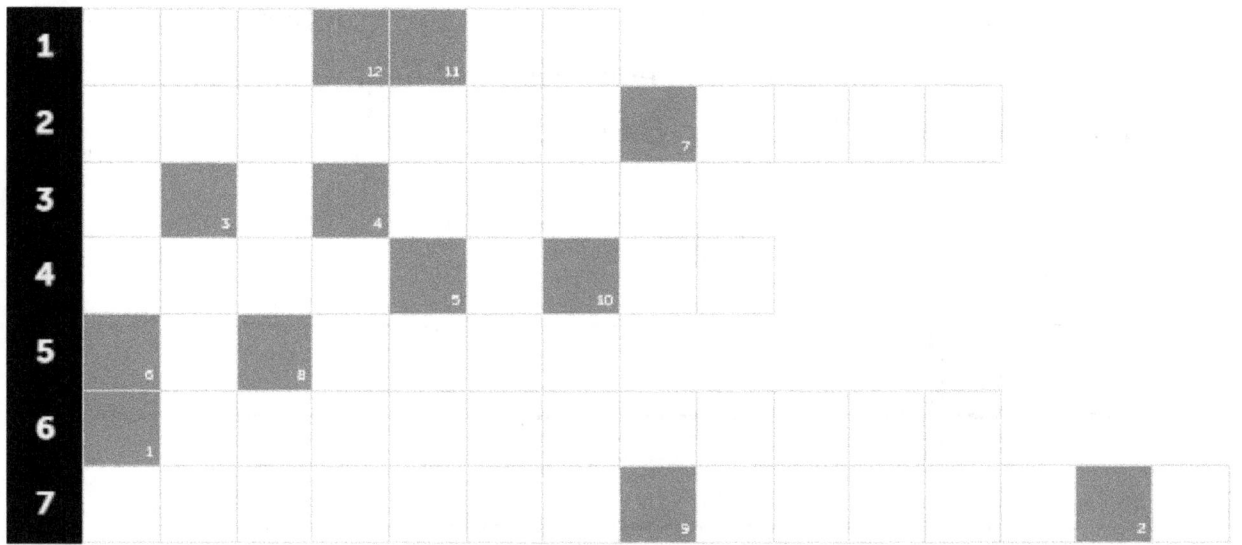

BONUS WORD

Unscramble Words

1) srctesa
2) rayadcameawd
3) xlomcmal
4) skweofhar
5) htrpena
6) zoeyondhboth
7) laiohtxtwgeaine

Directions: This is the WGLT Challenge. Solve the cryptogram. As the puzzle solver, you need to find which number belongs to which character. And this can be pretty challenging! You will need to match the number with the letter. There are some letters given to you below. This will help you solve the other words and unlock more characters. **Good Luck.**

170

John Singleton

January 6, 1968 – April 28, 2019
FILM DIRECTOR / SCREENWRITER

171

LEFT BLANK ON PURPOSE

John Singleton

John Singleton

John Singleton

John Singleton

John Singleton

John Singleton

Directions: read the bio below and answer the following questions.

Hi, my name is John Singleton. I was born on January 6, 1968, in Los Angeles, CA. I graduated from Blair High School. I received my bachelor's degree in screenwriting from the University of Southern California's School of Cinematic Arts. I won three writing awards from the university, which led to a contract with Creative Artists Agency. I also became a member of the Kappa Alpha Psi fraternity. In 1991, I made my film debut with Boyz n the Hood, which stars Cuba Gooding, Jr., Angela Bassett, Ice Cube and Laurence Fishburne. I became the youngest person ever to be nominated for Best Director at the age of 24 and the first African American to be nominated for the award. In 2002, the United States Library of Congress deemed my film "culturally significant" and selected it for preservation in the National Film Registry. Some of the films I directed include Rosewood, Poetic Justice, Baby Boy, Higher Learning, Shaft, 2 Fast 2 Furious and Four Brothers.

1. What is the name of my fraternity?
    A. Omega Psi Phi
    B. Alpha Phi Alpha
    C. Kappa Alpha Psi
2. What film was my debut into Hollywood?
    A. Poetic Justice
    B. Boyz n the Hood
    C. 2 Fast 2 Furious
3. I was the youngest person ever nominated for?
    A. Best Director
    B. Best Actor
    C. Best Supporting Actor

Directions: Find the words associated with John's life and career.

```
F V G A V F P R O D U C E R Z Y G U
U I U O S U O I R U F 2 T S A F 2 A
Z D L Q D T M U K H N F Y K F K Q Q
S U N M T F A H S Y R S O I R N F Q
O X W E M Y R H J T P O B C V S D S
K Q I T I A V R U P Y Y Z G Y I Z
K R J P X W K H R O D H B L D O N Z
T Z I G M E I E N P T A A R I T T V
W Y V Z Q S O I R Y S C B C N B K Y
W T L A N O K H A B N Y E A Y S P R
Q I Y Q Z J H J W A L K W R T A M E
K H T U O X Y Q W M E V J I I M U M
I C N C I Q W M L Y G V U X B D G D
A F O U R B R O T H E R S G Z X K Q
Z Y K J U R U K A H S C A P U T P D
S D L N V F G Y T V O M Z I X E W O
U P O E T I C J U S T I C E N G X V
W F T X O Y F O Q C K R X H H Z U C
```

Find These Words

FILMMAKER   BABYBOY   DIRECTOR
FOURBROTHERS 2FAST2FURIOUS   SHAFT
POETICJUSTICE PRODUCER   TUPACSHAKUR

Directions: Read and answer the questions. These are your opinions so the answers will vary.

Can you name a musician who sings and plays an instrument at the same time?

Who is your favorite actor or actress and why?

Can you name an actor or actress who has won an Academy Award?

Directions: Read and answer the questions below. There are clues in the puzzle to help you. Try and solve the cryptic message.

Clue for cryptic message: John co-created this television drama.

Questions

1) John created the film "Poetic ____," to give a voice to young African-American women.
2) Boyz N The Hood was based off of John's life ___ up in L.A.
3) John was the first African-American to be nominated for Best ____.
4) John would ___ animated stories in a notepad with his favorite superheroes.
5) John has earned himself a star on Hollywood's Walk of ____.
6) John directed the iconic 9-minute music video "Remember the Time" for ___ Jackson.
7) John was inspired to be a director after watching the making of ____ Encounters of the Third Kind with Steven Spielberg.
8) John at one time considered pursuing computer science at University of Southern ____.

Directions: This is the WGLT Challenge. Solve the cryptogram. As the puzzle solver, you need to find which number belongs to which character. And this can be pretty challenging! You will need to match the number with the letter. There are some letters given to you below. This will help you solve the other words and unlock more characters. **Good Luck.**

178

Viola Davis

Viola Davis

August 11, 1965 – PRESENT
ACTRESS / PRODUCER

179

LEFT BLANK ON PURPOSE

Viola Davis

Viola Davis

Viola Davis

Viola Davis

Viola Davis

Viola Davis

Directions: read the bio below and answer the following questions.

Hi, my name is Viola Davis. I was born on August 11, 1965, in Matthews, SC. I graduated from Central Falls High School. I received my bachelor's degree in theater from Rhode Island College. I attended the Juilliard School for four years. In 1992, I starred in my first professional stage role in an off-Broadway production of William Shakespeare's comedy As You Like It. I played Denis and the play was held at the Delacorte Theatre. In 1996, I made my film debut as a nurse in the film The Substance of Fire. In 2011, I had my breakout role as Aibileen Clark in the film adaptation of Kathryn Stockett's novel The Help. Some of the films and TV shows that I have acted in are Get on Up, How to Get Away with Murder, Blackhat, Fences, Suicide Squad, Widows and The Unforgivable. In 2015, I became the first Black actress to win the Primetime Emmy Award for Outstanding Lead Actress in a Drama Series. In 2020, I became the most-nominated Black actress in Oscar history with my nomination for Ma Rainey in Ma Rainey's Black Bottom.

1. What Performing Arts school did I attend?
    A. NYU Tisch School of the Arts—Drama and Dance
    B. The Juilliard School—Drama and Dance
    C. UNC School of the Arts—Drama and Dance
2. What year did I make my debut in film?
    A. 1996
    B. 1992
    C. 2011
3. In 202 I became the most-nominated black actress in?
    A. Emmy history
    B. Golden Globe history
    C. Oscar history

Directions: Answer the questions, to solve the crossword puzzle. You can use the internet if you get stuck on any question.

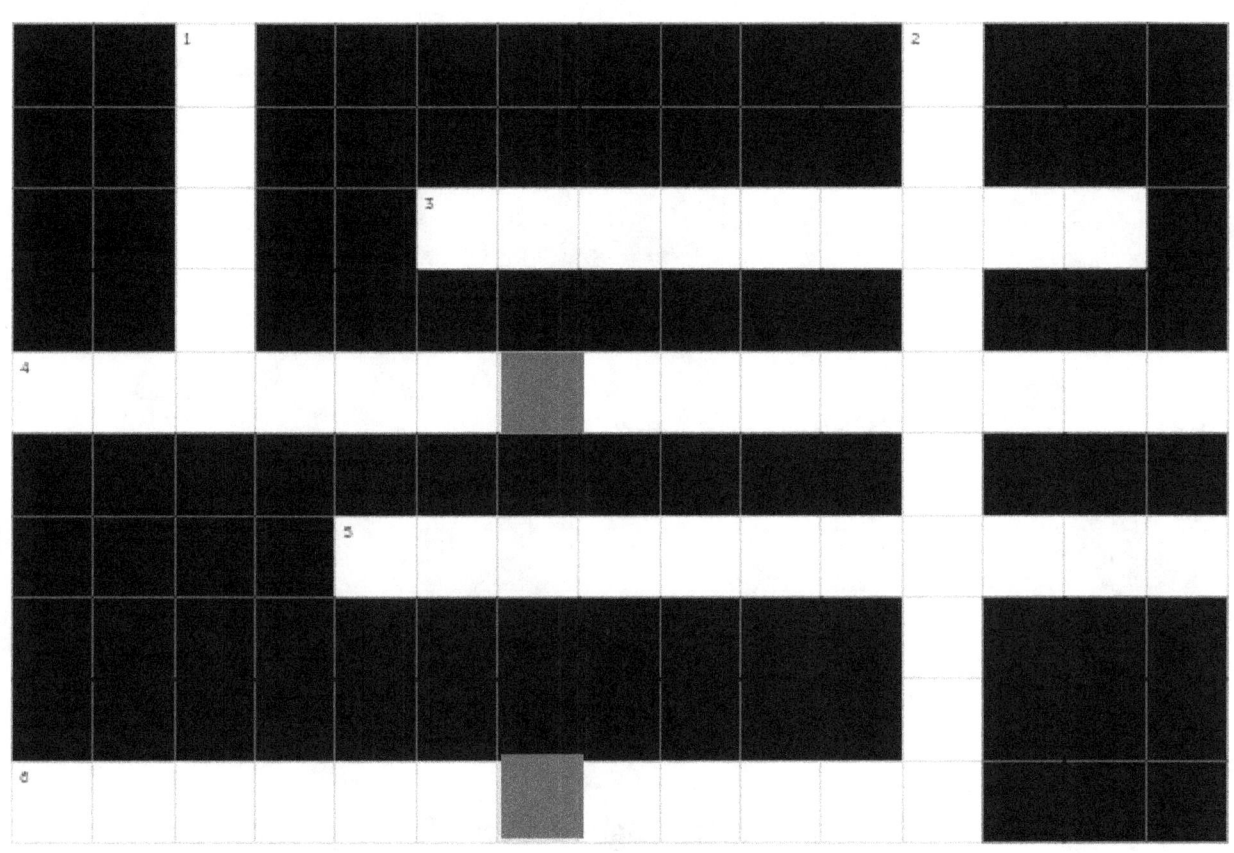

Across

3) Viola received a star on the _____ Walk of Fame.
4) Viola was inducted into The Academy of _____ Arts and Sciences.
5) Viola was listed as one of the 100 Most _____ People in the world.
6) Viola is the only African-American to achieve the _____ of Acting at this time 2022.

Down

1) Viola's film breakthrough came with her role as a troubled mother in the 2008 drama _____, for which she received her first Academy Award nomination for Best Supporting Actress.
2) Viola co-founded a production company called JuVee _____.

Directions: Read and answer the questions. These are your opinions so the answers will vary.

Have you ever watched a movie that made you cry? If so, which one?

What is your favorite TV show and why?

Can you name a TV show that is no longer on the air but you still enjoy watching?

Directions: Unscramble the words below about Viola. See if you can get the bonus word.

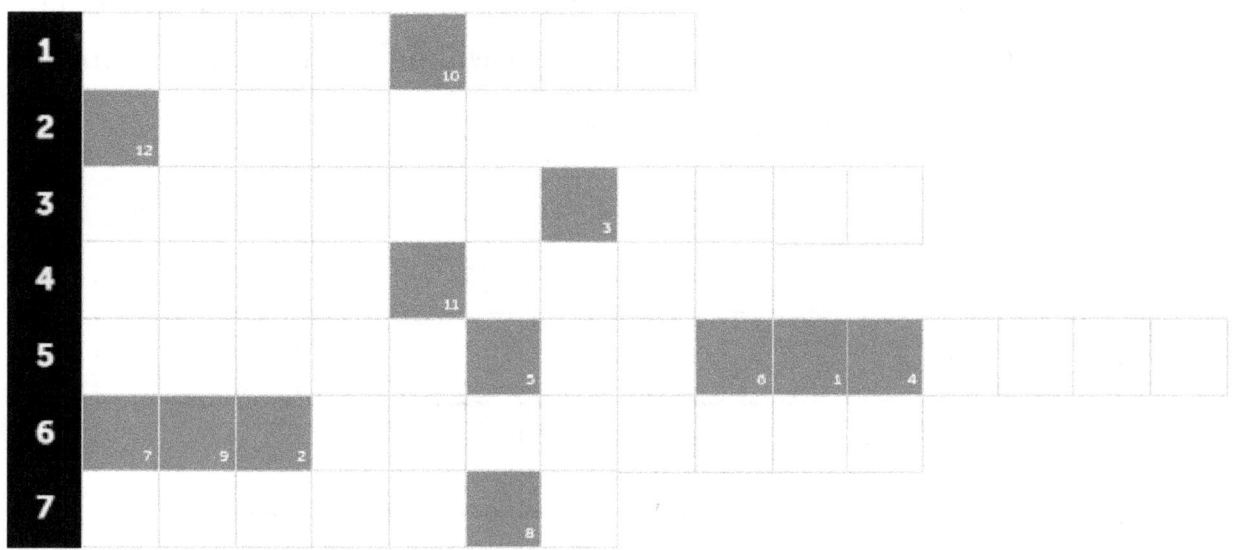

BONUS WORD

Unscramble Words

1) pudrecro   2) ubdot   3) gmhatnusrhi
4) maedmaryw   5) iouilcshalljdor   6) aeqisrlhtgu
7) crsaest

Directions: This is the WGLT Challenge. Solve the cryptogram. As the puzzle solver, you need to find which number belongs to which character. And this can be pretty challenging! You will need to match the number with the letter. There are some letters given to you below. This will help you solve the other words and unlock more characters. **Good Luck.**

December 25, 1907 – November 18, 1994
CONDUCTOR / SINGER / DANCER

187

LEFT BLANK ON PURPOSE

Cabell Calloway

Cabell Calloway

Cabell Calloway

Cabell Calloway

Cabell Calloway

Cabell Calloway

Directions: read the bio below and answer the following questions.

Hi, my name is Cabell Calloway III. I was born on December 25, 1907, in Rochester, NY. I graduated from Frederick Douglass High School. When my sister became an accomplished bandleader, I was inspired to enter show business. I performed as a singer, drummer and master of ceremonies at Sunset Café. I met and performed with Louis Armstrong, who taught me to sing in the scat style. In 1931, my band Cab Calloway and His Orchestra substituted for the Duke Ellington Orchestra at the Cotton Club while Ellington's band was on tour. Our popularity led to us being offered a permanent position. We performed twice a week for radio broadcasts on NBC. I was the first African American to have a nationally syndicated radio show. In 1931, I recorded my most famous song, "Minnie the Moocher." It was the first single record by an African American to sell a million copies. I performed songs in the Betty Boop cartoons in 1932 and in 1933, I performed "Minnie the Moocher," "Snow-White," and "The Old Man of the Mountain."

1. Who taught me how to sing in scat style?
   A. Duke Ellington
   B. Betty Boop
   C. Louis Armstrong
2. I was the first African American to have a?
   A. Record Deal
   B. Nationally Syndicated Radio Show
   C. My own Orchestra
3. My Song Minnie the Moocher was the first single record?
   A. To sell a million copies
   B. To reach #1 on the Billboard 100
   C. To be used in a cartoon

Directions: Find the words associated with Cabell's life and career.

```
J N T G M G M V F G D L M S D O I X
H F H N J M Q U K A T J E T N L I Y
C R E C A I Y F B H Q S W L O B U S
H G B P Z N J A Y X N T O O W S H T
H K L I Z N D A N C E R J R G Y I O
F Q U M H I X B E T T Y B O O P - R
O R E C A E I J X E I O U U F M D M
H A S I L T O J L C M V D Q U R E Y
F M B W L H Q W Y G J R P F Z E - W
V B R M O E N M Q F V Y X V H D H E
E N O B F M W V M S S N C L I A I A
M Z T Q F O P S Y M K H D W X E - T
D L H J A O Y U N Q A L Z P M L D H
H S E H M C J O M K C T E S V D E E
B C R N E H P O Z V V X H W O N - R
T Q S K J E T O Z D X M T R V A H A
D C N S F R W L H D D P Q S I B O P
C O Y Z A M L Z C O N D U C T O R T
```

Find These Words

BANDLEADER
CONDUCTOR
DANCER
HI-DE-HI-DE-HO
JAZZHALLOFFAME
MINNIETHEMOOCHER
THEBLUESBROTHERS
STORMYWEATHER
BETTYBOOP

Directions: Read and answer the questions. These are your opinions so the answers will vary.

Who is your favorite cartoon character and why?

Can you name a famous entertainer who makes you laugh?

Have you ever seen a play? If so, which one?

Directions: Read and answer the questions below. There are clues in the puzzle to help you. Try and solve the cryptic message.

Clue for cryptic message: Cab performed this genre.

Questions

1) President Clinton presented Cab Calloway with a National Medal of the ___.
2) Cab studied ___ at Crane University but music was his real passion.
3) Cab was inducted into the ___ Band and Jazz Hall of Fame.
4) Cab was a regular performer at the ___ Club as the bandleader of Cab Calloway and his Orchestra.
5) Louis Armstrong mentored and tutored Cab in the art of scat ___.

Directions: This is the WGLT Challenge. Solve the cryptogram. As the puzzle solver, you need to find which number belongs to which character. And this can be pretty challenging! You will need to match the number with the letter. There are some letters given to you below. This will help you solve the other words and unlock more characters. **Good Luck.**

194

Dorothy Jean Dandridge

November 9, 1922 – September 8, 1965
ACTRESS / SINGER

LEFT BLANK ON PURPOSE

Dorothy Jean Dandridge

Dorothy Jean Dandridge

Dorothy Jean Dandridge

Dorothy Jean Dandridge

Dorothy Jean Dandridge

Dorothy Jean Dandridge

Directions: read the bio below and answer the following questions.

Hi, my name is Dorothy Dandridge. I was born on November 9, 1922, in Cleveland, OH. I started performing at a young age with my sister Vivian. We had a song-and-dance act and we were called The Wonder Children. We toured the Chitlin' Circuit until the Great Depression started. We relocated and in 1934, we changed our act's name to The Dandridge Sisters. Our friend Etta Jones also joined our group. We performed in several high-profile New York nightclubs, including the Cotton Club and the Apollo Theater. In 1935, I made my first film appearance when I was 13 in an Our Gang comedy short, "Teacher's Beau." In 1954, I starred in the film Carmen Jones as Carmen. I was nominated for an Academy Award for Best Actress, which made me the first African American to be nominated for a leading role. I also became the first Black woman to be featured on the cover of Life that same year. In 1955, I became the first Black performer to open at the Empire Room at New York's Waldorf-Astoria hotel. This opened the door for other African Americans to perform there.

1. Our group name before The Dandridge Sisters was?
   A. The Wonder Children
   B. The Wonder Kids
   C. The Wonder Sisters
2. What year did I make my film debut?
   A. 1934
   B. 1935
   C. 1936
3. I was the first African American nominated for?
   A. Golden Globe for Best Actress
   B. Academy Award for Best Actress
   C. Emmy for Best Actress

Directions: Answer the questions, to solve the crossword puzzle. You can use the internet if you get stuck on any question.

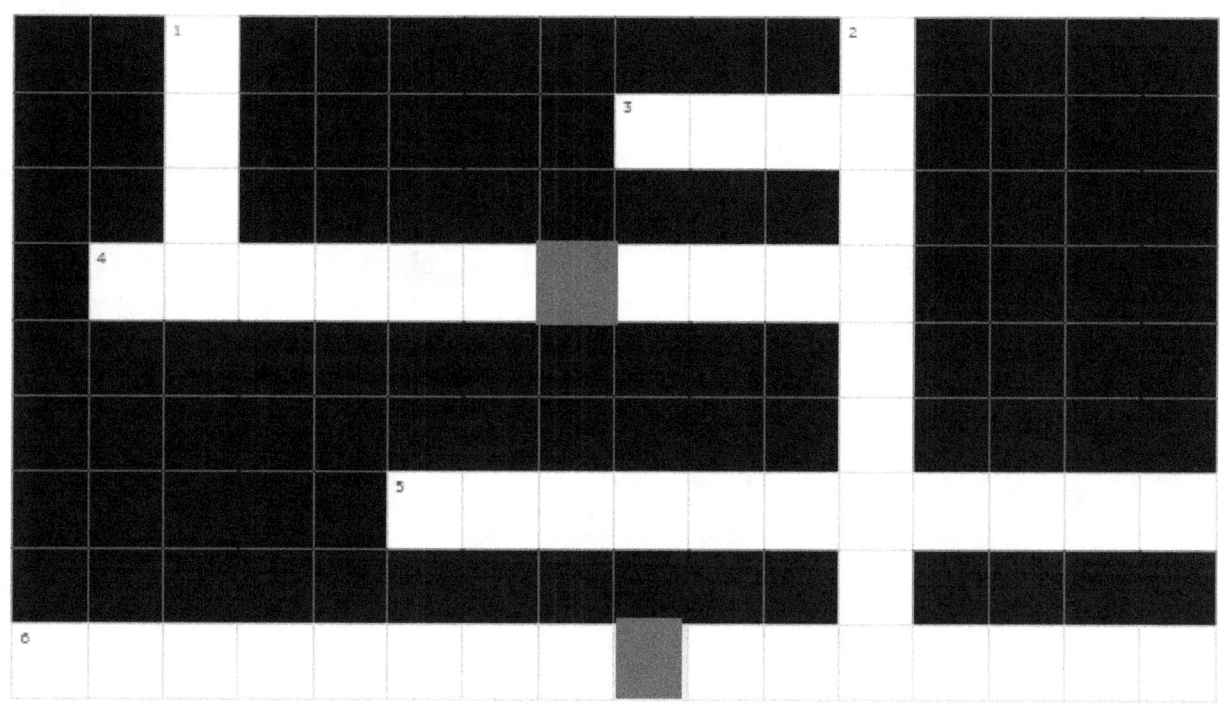

Across

3) Dorothy became the first black woman featured on the cover of ___.

4) Dorothy appeared in a film "_____," opposite Harry Belafonte.

5) Dorothy appeared in the film "___ Choo Choo" and was the first time she performed with the Nicholas Brothers.

6) Dorothy and her sister toured on the _____ as The Wonder Children.

Down

1) Dorothy's first credited film role was in ___ Shall Die in 1940.

2) Dorothy success as a _____ at the New York's Waldorf-Astoria hotel led to the hotel booking other black performers

Directions: Read and answer the questions. These are your opinions so the answers will vary.

Can you name a famous Broadway actor or actress?

Who is your favorite superhero and why?

Can you name a famous voice actor?

Directions: Unscramble the words below about Dorothy. See if you can get the bonus word.

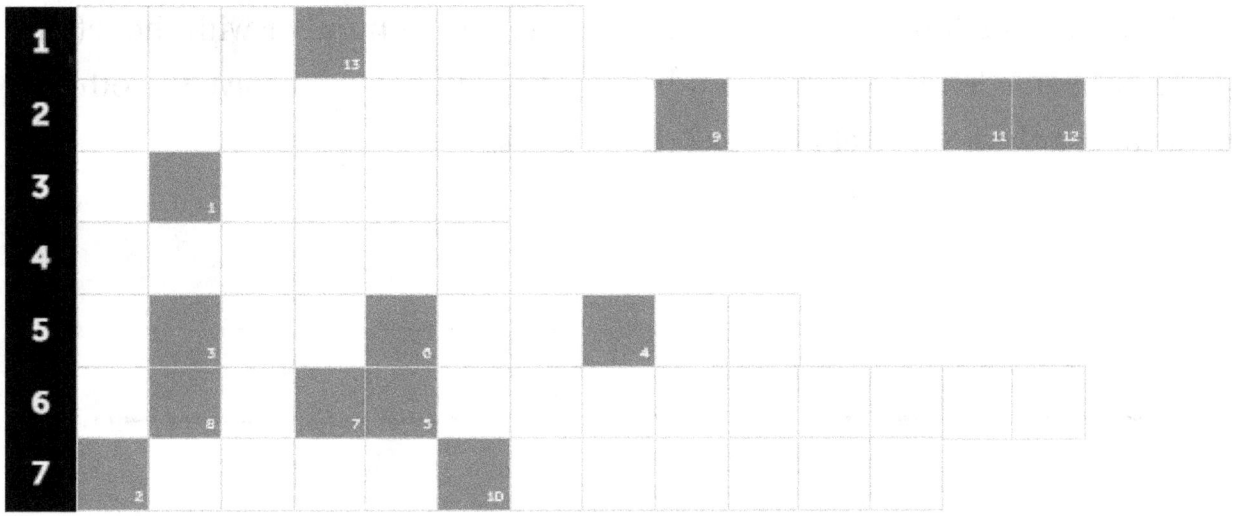

BONUS WORD

Unscramble Words

1) reacsst
2) iedsgarsenddrtis
3) adrenc
4) riegns
7) nopdgysbrsae
5) onuoccttlb
6) itciulhcritinc

Directions: This is the WGLT Challenge. Solve the cryptogram. As the puzzle solver, you need to find which number belongs to which character. And this can be pretty challenging! You will need to match the number with the letter. There are some letters given to you below. This will help you solve the other words and unlock more characters. **Good Luck.**

202

1. What was the name of my High School?
   A. Charles Evans Hughes High School
   B. Bronx High School for the Visual Arts
   C. Morris High School
2. What year did I start acting?
   A. 1950
   B. 1955
   C. 1956
3. I'm known as the person who?
   A. Would take any role
   B. Would take positive images of Black women
   C. Would only work on Broadway

Cicely Tyson
Answers

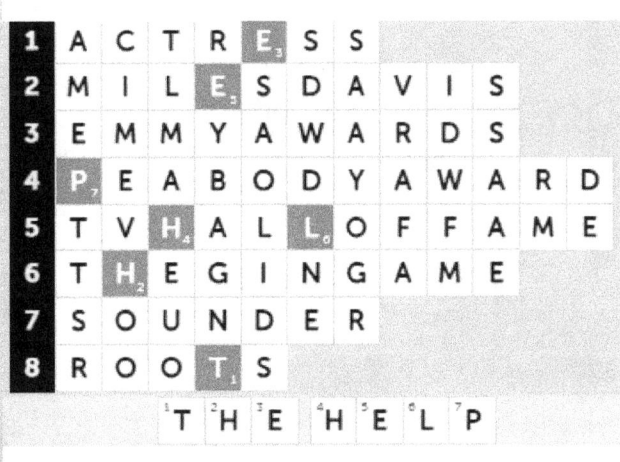
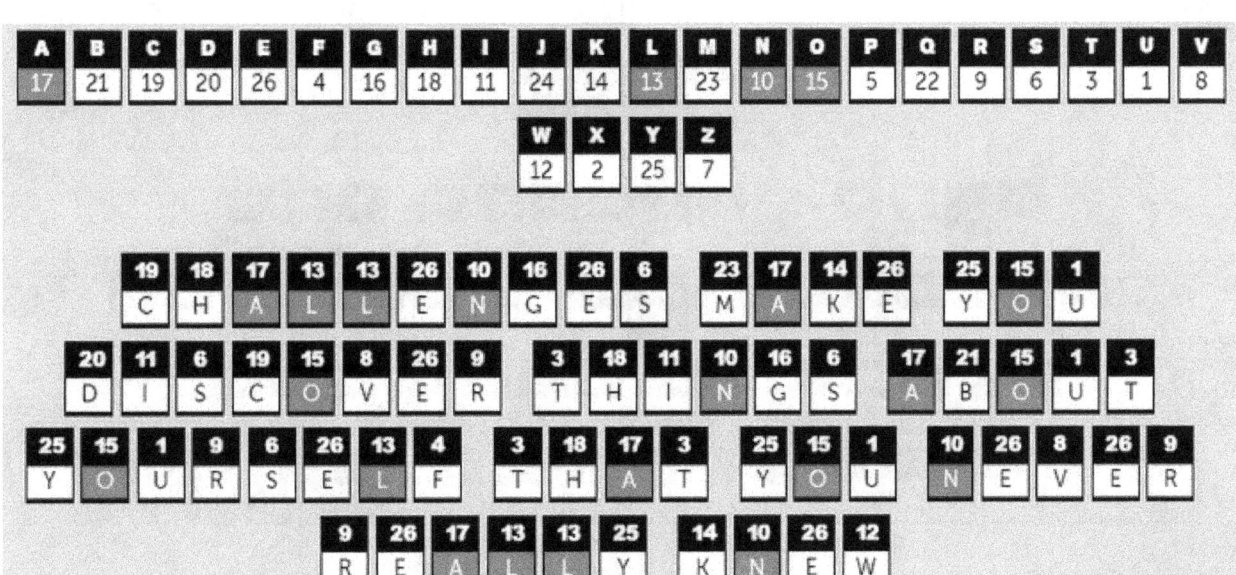

203

James Earl Jones Answers

1. What was the name of the college I graduate from?
   A. University of Mississippi
   B. University of Michigan
   C. University of Maryland
2. What year did I become an Army Ranger?
   A. 1953
   B. 1955
   C. 1957
3. I won a Tony Award for what?
   A. The movie The Great White Hope
   B. The play The Great White Hope
   C. The radio version of The Great White Hope

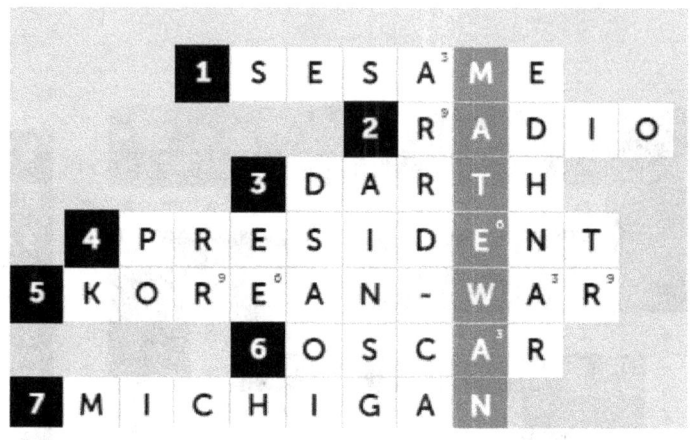

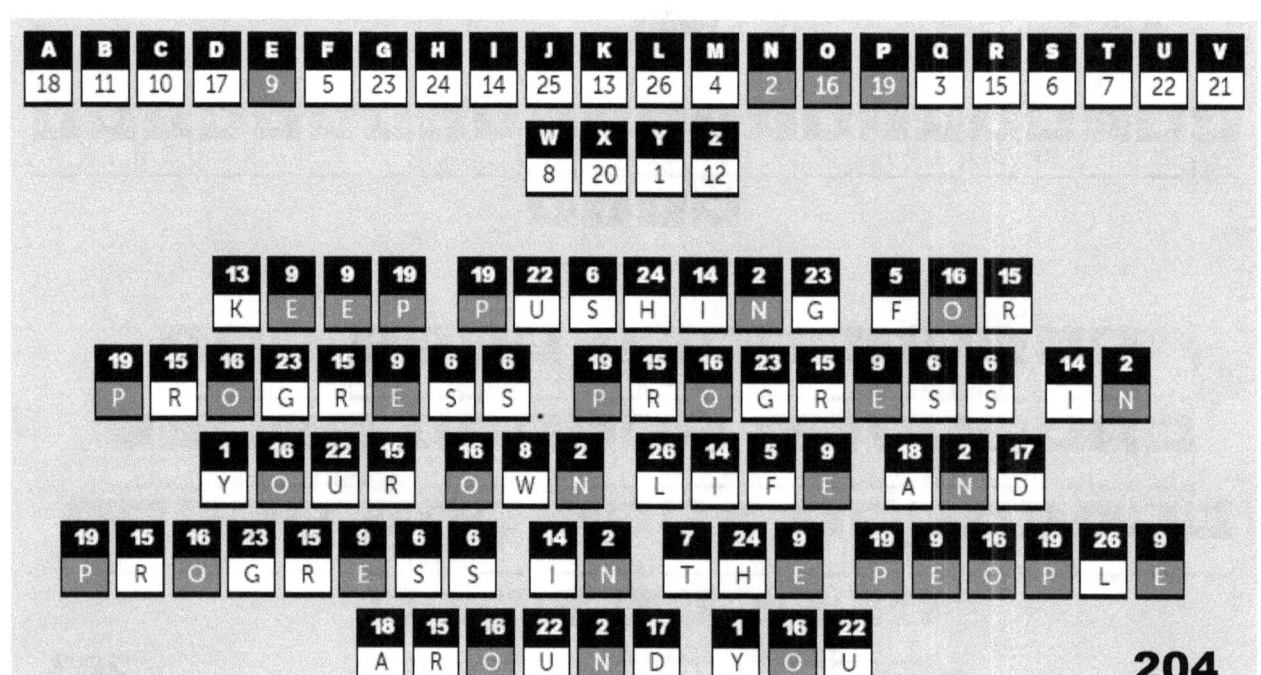

"KEEP PUSHING FOR PROGRESS. PROGRESS IN YOUR OWN LIFE AND PROGRESS IN THE PEOPLE AROUND YOU."

204

1. Which pageant title is not one that I have won?
   A. Miss Black New Jersey
   B. Miss Press Photographer
   C. Miss Black New York
2. How old was I when I started acting?
   A. 17
   B. 22
   C. 25
3. I was the first African American woman to win?
   A. An Academy Award for Best Actress
   B. A Golden Globe Award for Best Actress
   C. A Tony for Best Actress

Gail Fisher
Answers

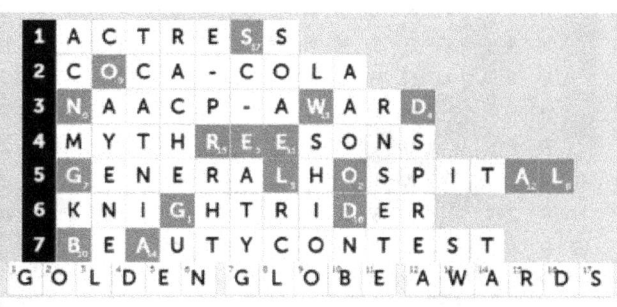
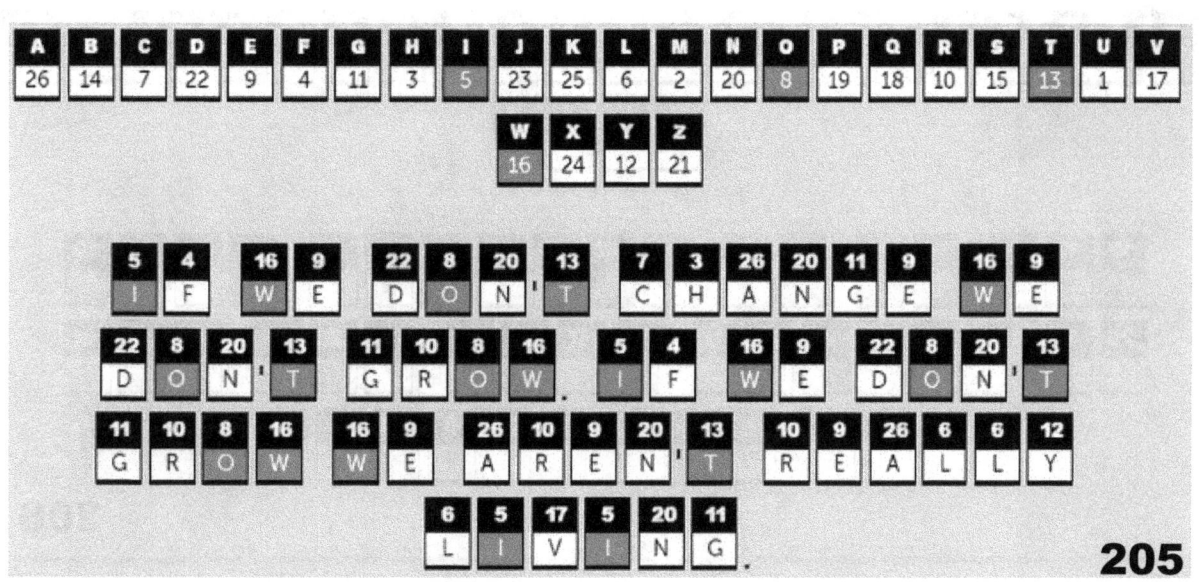

IF WE DON'T CHANGE WE DON'T GROW. IF WE DON'T GROW WE AREN'T REALLY LIVING.

Sidney Poitier Answers

1. What branch of service was I enlisted in?
   A. Navy
   B. Army
   C. Marine Corps
2. What year did I help found the CNA?
   A. 1948
   B. 1950
   C. 1947
3. I was the first African American actor to do what?
   A. Win a Golden Globe award
   B. Win an Academy Award
   C. Win an Emmy award

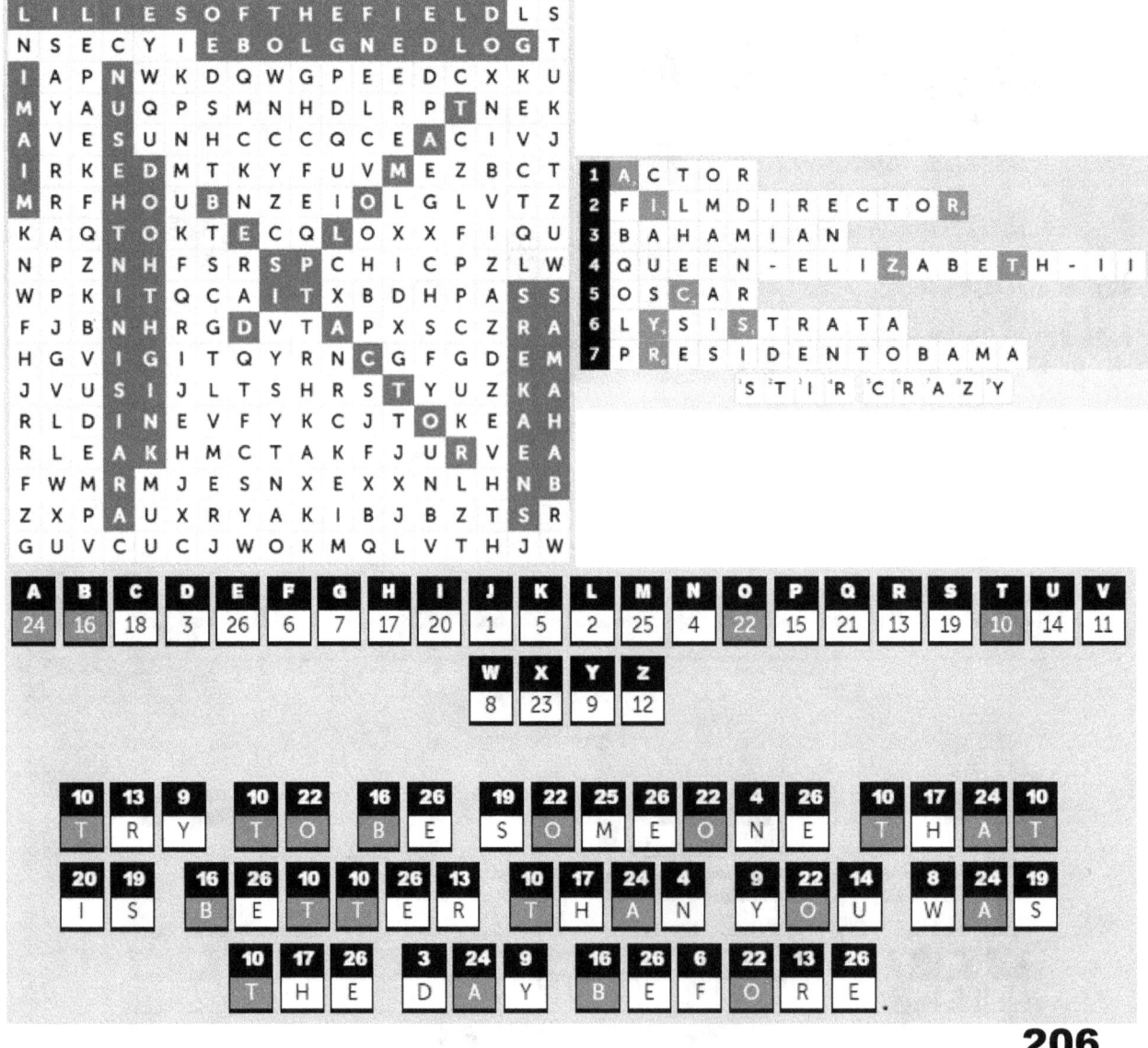

1. ACTOR
2. FILM DIRECTOR
3. BAHAMIAN
4. QUEEN-ELIZABETH-II
5. OSCAR
6. LYSISTRATA
7. PRESIDENT OBAMA

STIR CRAZY

"TRY TO BE SOMEONE THAT IS BETTER THAN YOU WAS THE DAY BEFORE."

206

1. What is the name of my sorority?
   A. Delta Sigma Theta
   B. Zeta Phi Beta
   C. Alpha Kappa Alpha
2. What was my first TV appearance as an actress?
   A. One Life to Live
   B. Delvecchio
   C. The Cosby Show
3. I was the first black actress to win?
   A. Tony Award for Best Actress in a Play
   B. Emmy Award for Best Actress
   C. Academy Award for Best Actress

Phylicia Ayers-Allen
Answers

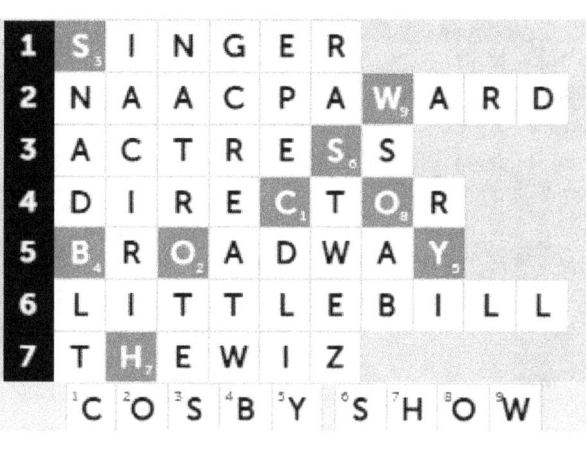

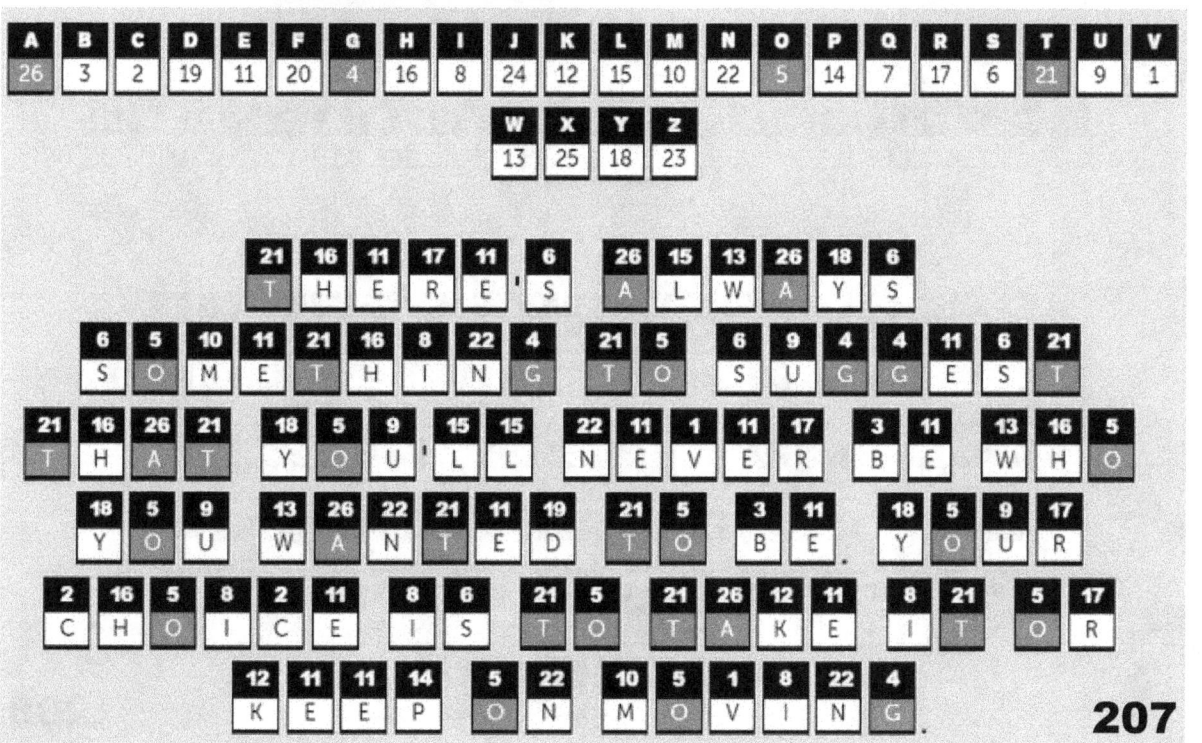

THERE'S ALWAYS SOMETHING TO SUGGEST THAT YOU'LL NEVER BE WHO YOU WANTED TO BE. YOUR CHOICE IS TO TAKE IT OR KEEP ON MOVING.

207

Chadwick Boseman
Answers

1. What is the name of the HBCU that I attended?
   A. Alcorn State University
   B. Howard University
   C. Morehouse University
2. What year did I start working in Television?
   A. 2002
   B. 2004
   C. 2003
3. I played in the Marvel movie Black Panther as?
   A. M'Baku
   B. T'Challa
   C. Erik Killmonger

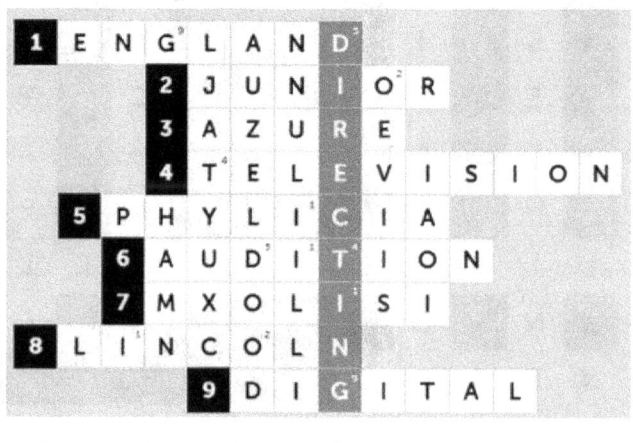

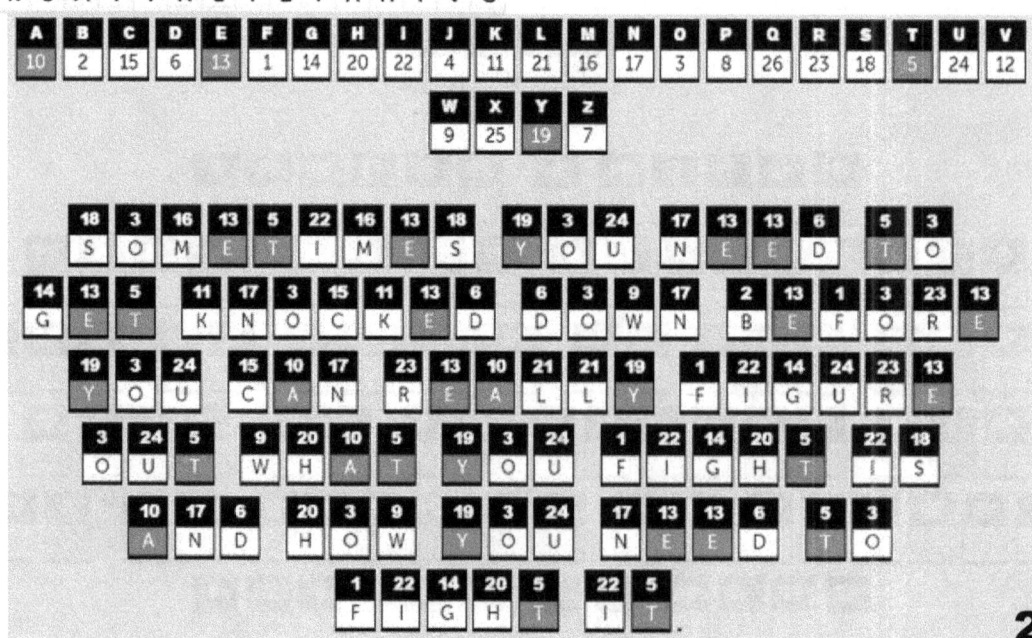

"SOMETIMES YOU NEED TO GET KNOCKED DOWN BEFORE YOU CAN REALLY FIGURE OUT WHAT YOU FIGHT IS AND HOW YOU NEED TO FIGHT IT."

208

1. What is the name of the HBCU I attended?
   A. Fisk University
   B. Spellman College
   C. Tennessee State University
2. What year was The Oprah Winfrey Show started?
   A. 1985
   B. 1986
   C. 1984
3. I was the first black woman?
   A. Millionaire
   B. Billionaire
   C. Trillionaire

Oprah Winfrey Answers

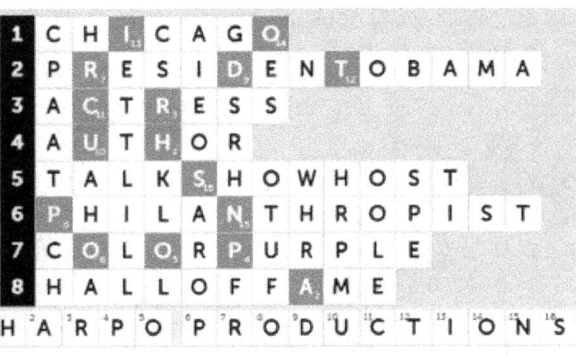
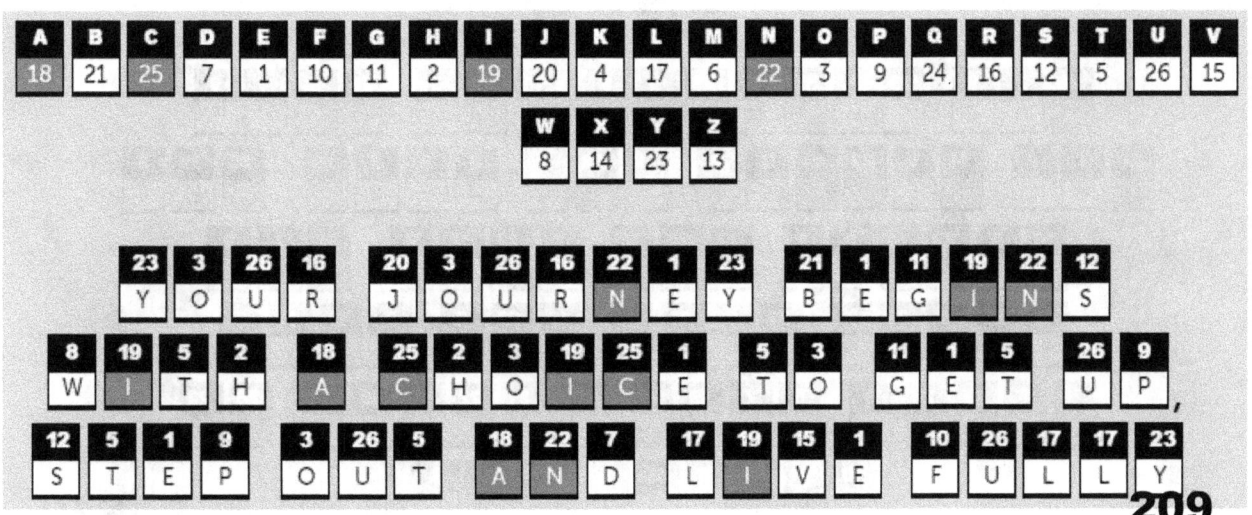

1. What college did I get my Bachelors degree from?
   A. Florida University
   B. Fordham University
   C. Texas Tech University
2. What show did I receive national attention from?
   A. St. Elsewhere
   B. Extra
   C. Mother goose a rappin' and rhymin' special
3. I won the Academy Award for Best Actor in what film?
   A. Glory
   B. Malcom X
   C. Training Day

Denzel Washington
Answers

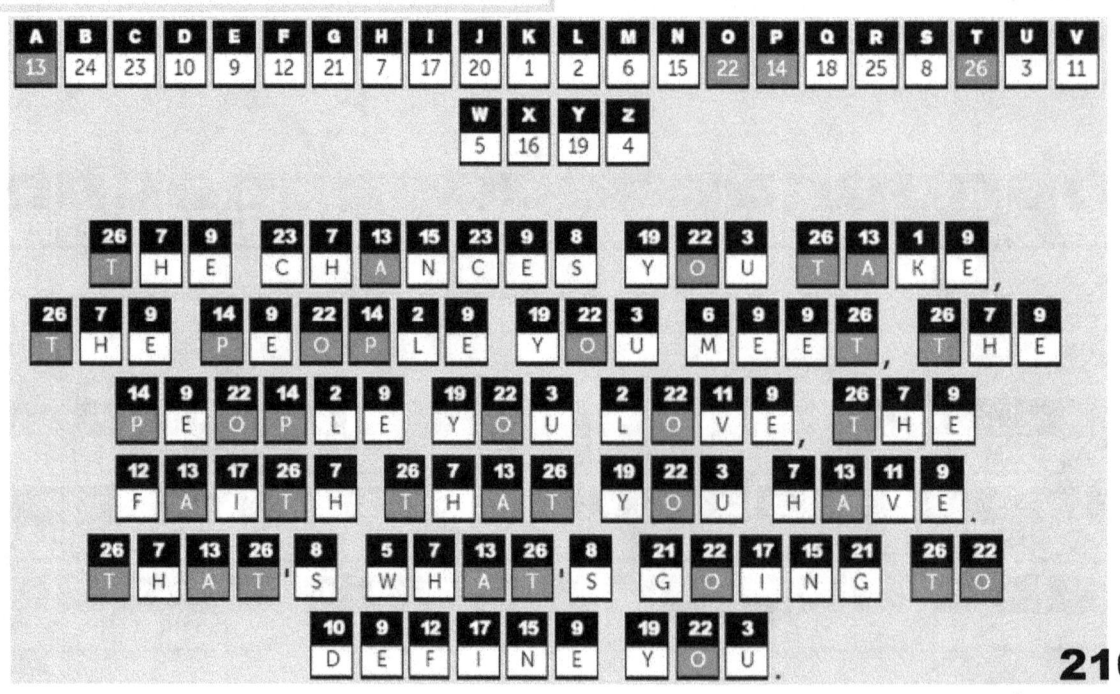

THE CHANCES YOU TAKE, THE PEOPLE YOU MEET, THE PEOPLE YOU LOVE, THE FAITH THAT YOU HAVE. THAT'S WHAT'S GOING TO DEFINE YOU.

210

1. What was my stage name on the radio?
   A. Mammy
   B. Hi-Hat Hattie
   C. Queenie
2. What year did I start working in films?
   A. 1935
   B. 1939
   C. 1932
3. I became the first African American to win?
   A. Oscar
   B. Emmy
   C. Golden Globe

Hattie McDaniel
Answers

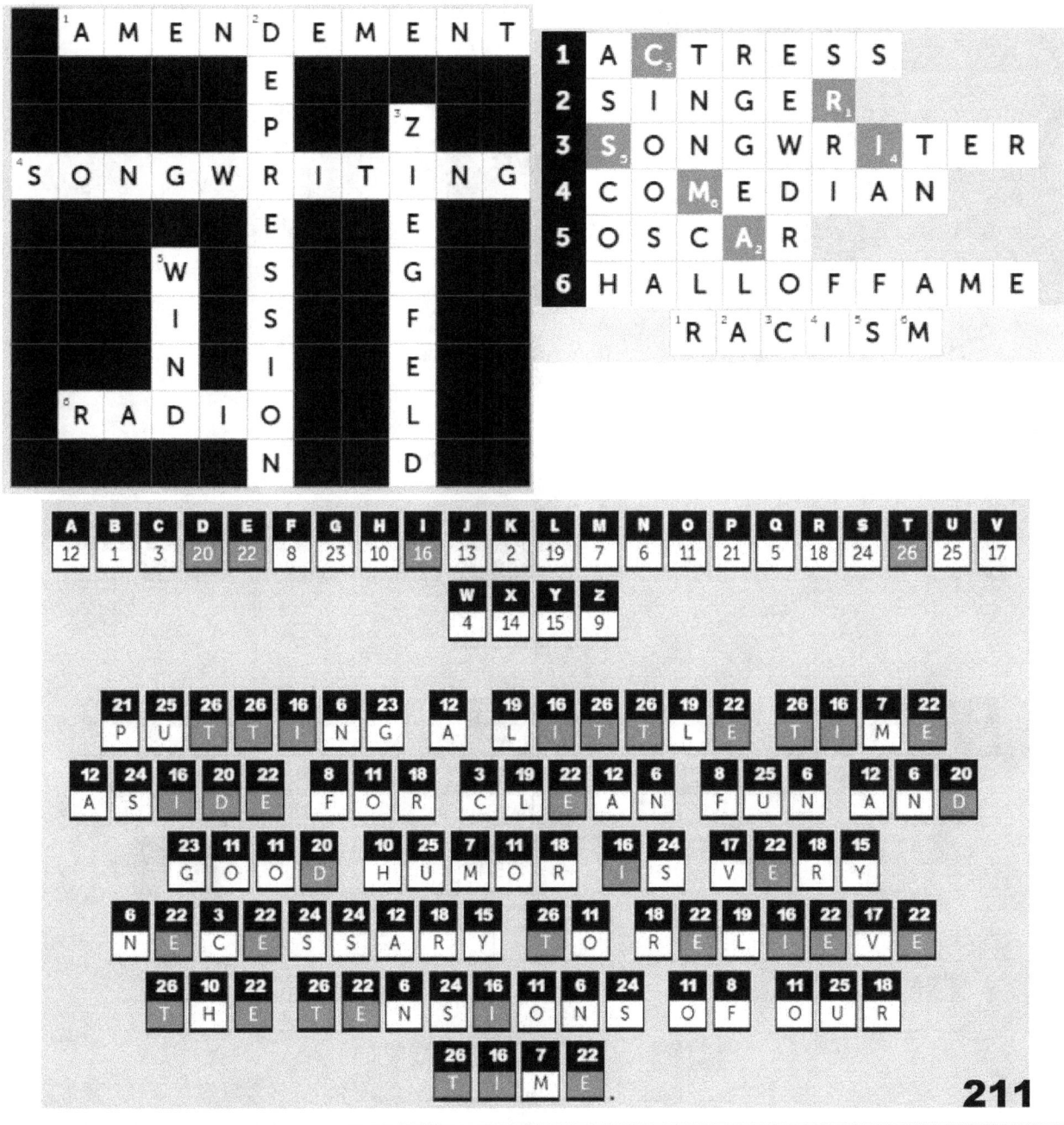

"PUTTING A LITTLE TIME ASIDE FOR CLEAN FUN AND GOOD HUMOR IS VERY NECESSARY TO RELIEVE THE TENSIONS OF OUR TIME."

1. What was the name of the HBCU that I graduated from?
   A. Clark University
   B. Morehouse College
   C. Fisk University
2. What year did I debut my first major film?
   A. 1988
   B. 1989
   C. 1986
3. Which film is not one of mine?
   A. Ghostwriter
   B. Malcolm X
   C. BlacKkKlansman

Shelton Jackson Lee
Answers

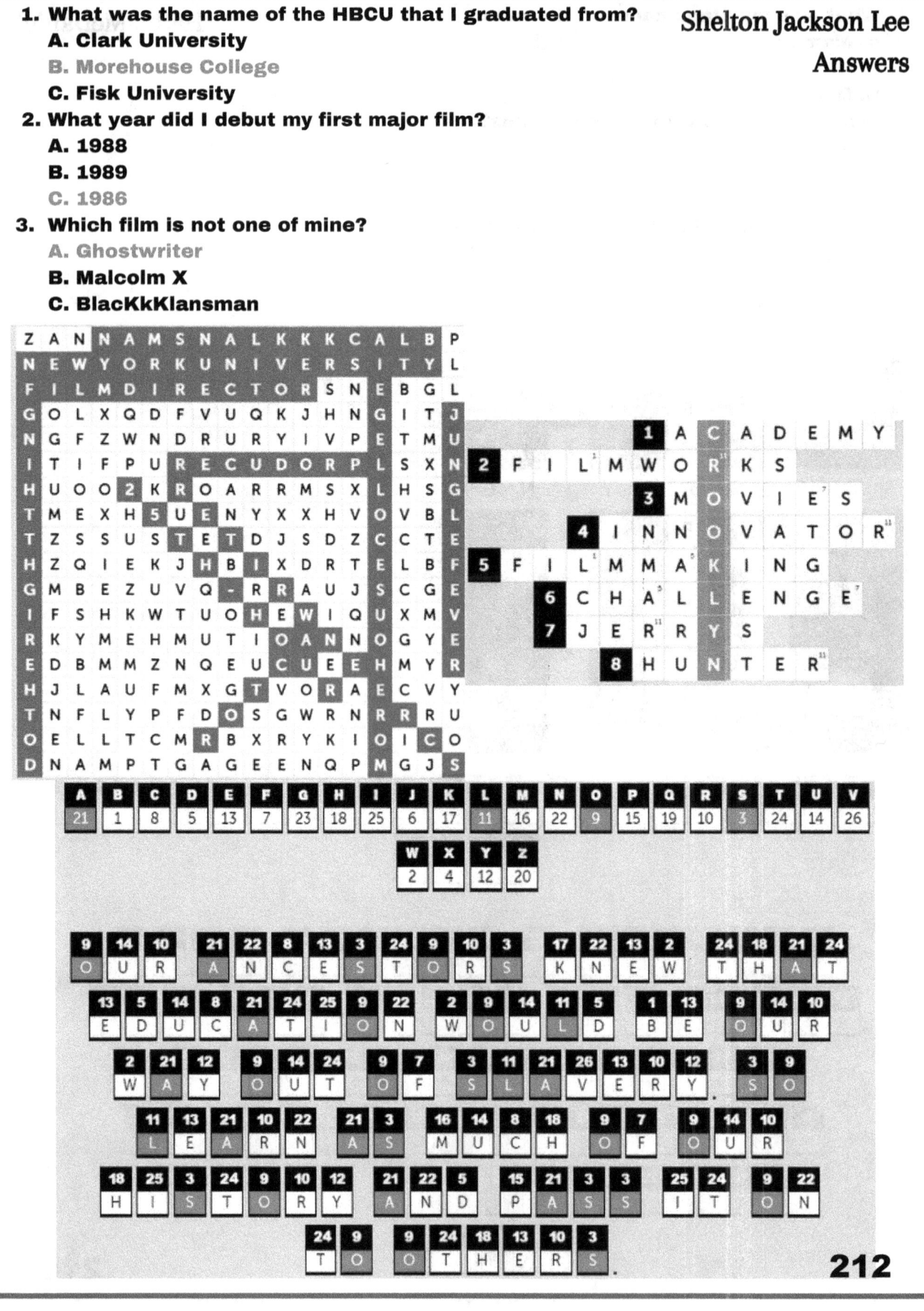

"OUR ANCESTORS KNEW THAT EDUCATION WOULD BE OUR WAY OUT OF SLAVERY. SO LEARN AS MUCH OF OUR HISTORY AND PASS IT ON TO OTHERS."

212

1. What was the name of my first TV show appearance?
   A. The Wedding
   B. The Simpsons
   C. Living Dolls
2. What year did I start working in the film industry?
   A. 1986
   B. 1991
   C. 1989
3. I was the first African American woman to win?
   A. Academy Award for Best Actress
   B. Academy Award for Best Supporting Actress
   C. Emmy Award for Best Actress

Halle Berry Answers

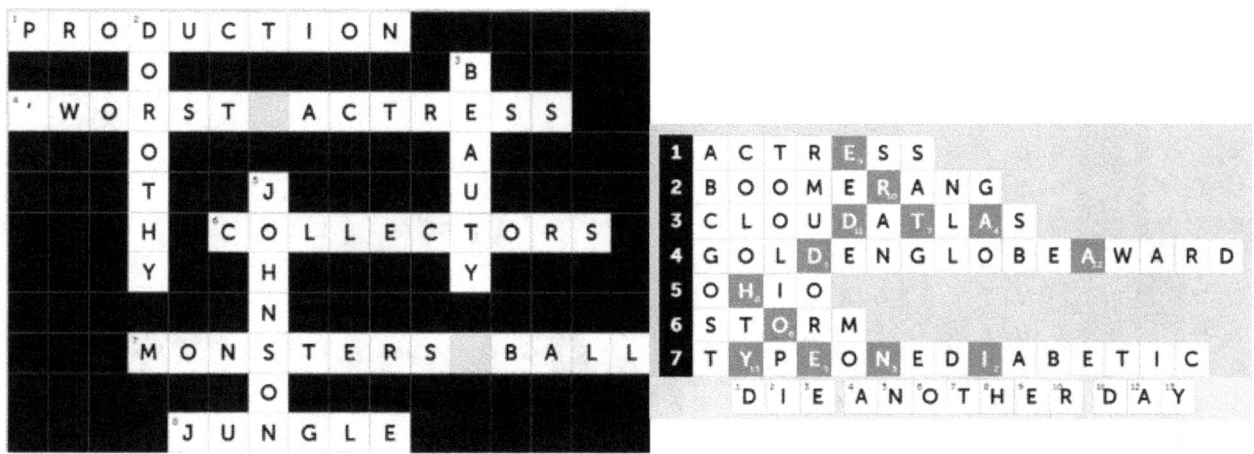

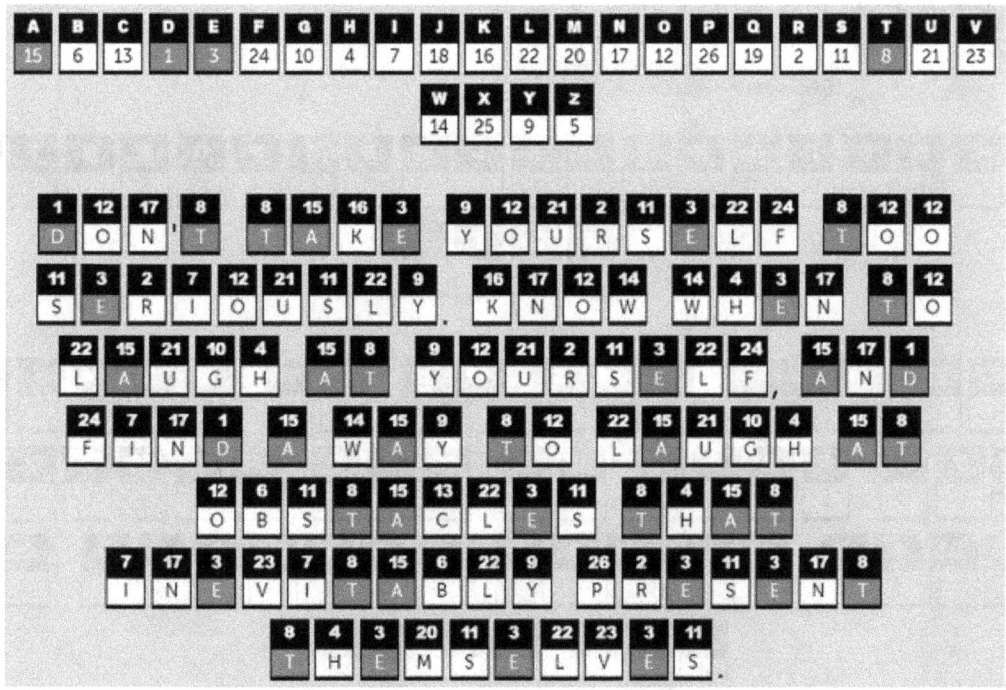

"DON'T TAKE YOURSELF TOO SERIOUSLY. KNOW WHEN TO LAUGH AT YOURSELF, AND FIND A WAY TO LAUGH AT OBSTACLES THAT INEVITABLY PRESENT THEMSELVES."

Tyler Perry Answers

1. What was my birth name?
   A. Tyler
   B. Emmitt
   C. Alex
2. What year did I do my first musical?
   A. 1993
   B. 1998
   C. 1992
3. Which of these films didn't I write, direct and produce?
   A. The Have and Have Nots
   B. Madea's Family Reunion
   C. Star Trek

1. FAME
2. OPRAH
3. DIRECTING
4. GOSPEL
5. CHANGED

ALL YOU CAN DO IS PLANT YOUR SEED IN THE GROUND, WATER IT AND BELIEVE IT CAN GROW.

214

1. What was the name of the first club I joined?
   A. Cafe Society
   B. Cafe Trocadero
   C. Cotton Club
2. What film did I debut for MGM?
   A. Panama Hattie
   B. Cabin in the Sky
   C. Duchess of Idaho
3. I was the first African-American woman to?
   A. be nominated for a Academy Award for Best Actress
   B. be nominated for a Emmy Award for Best Actress
   C. be nominated for a Tony Award for Best Actress

Lena Horne Answers

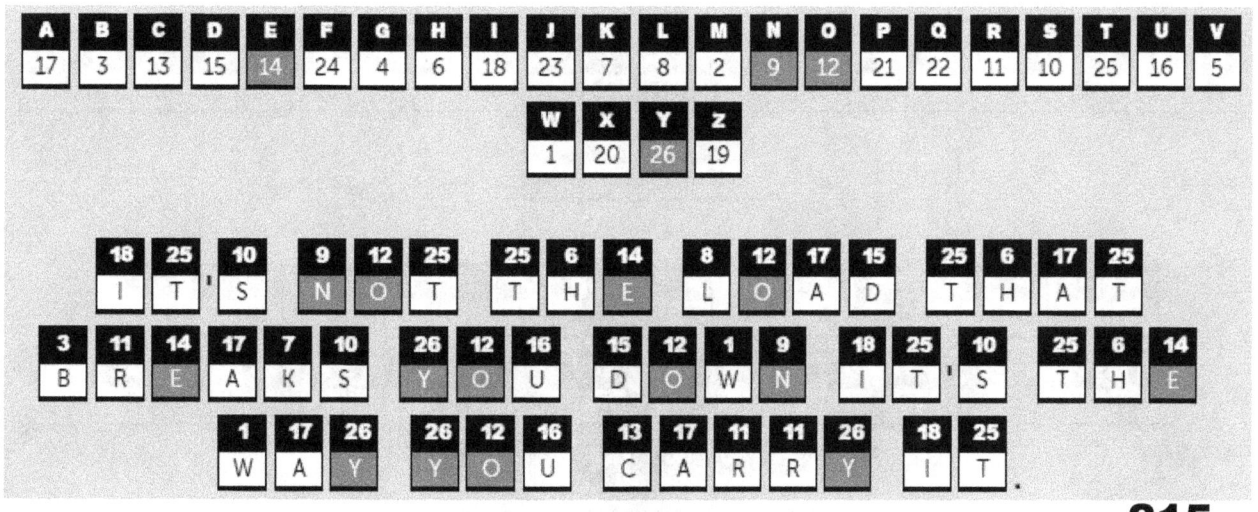

215

Fayard and Harold Nicholas
Answers

1. Where did we learn how to dance and sing?
   A. Dance School
   B. Singing School
   C. Self taught
2. What year did we make our Broadway debut?
   A. 1934
   B. 1932
   C. 1936
3. When we were 11 and 18 what club did we feature at?
   A. Cotton Club
   B. Standard
   C. Pearl

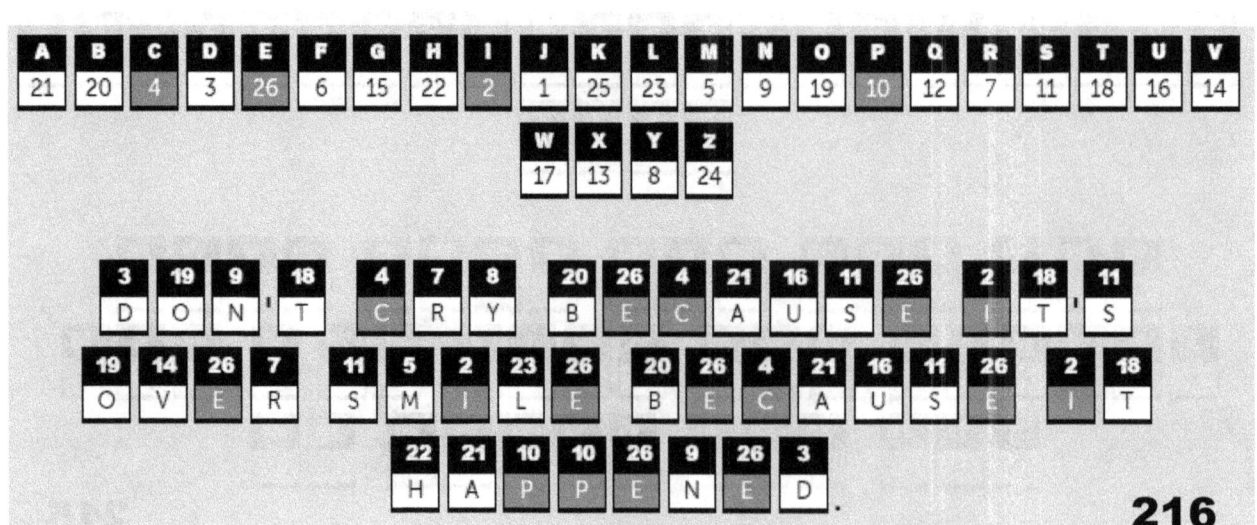

DON'T CRY BECAUSE IT'S OVER SMILE BECAUSE IT HAPPENED.

1. What was the name of the dance center I start at?
   A. ABT Studio Company
   B. San Pedro Dance Center
   C. San Francisco Ballet
2. I was first African American woman to dance what role?
   A. Swanilda in Coppélia at the Met.
   B. Birthday Offering at the Met
   C. Ratmansky's The Bright Stream at the Met
3. I became the first African-American woman to?
   A. be promoted to soloist in ABT
   B. be promoted to principal ballerina at NY City Ballet
   C. be promoted to principal ballerina at ABT

Misty Copeland
Answers

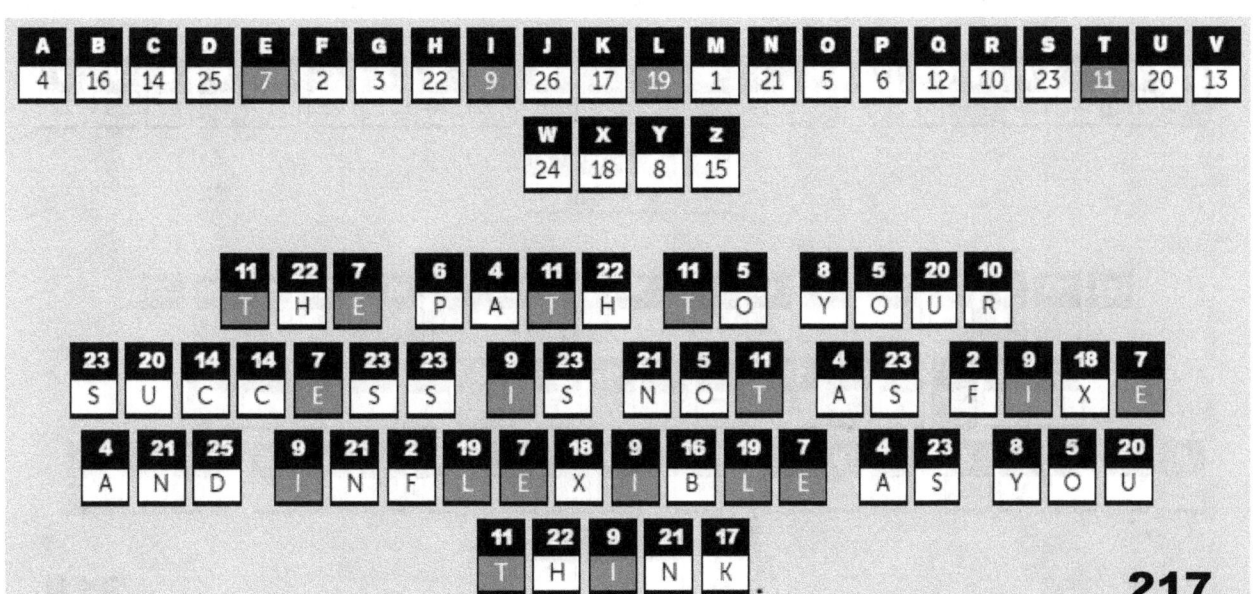

"THE PATH TO YOUR SUCCESS IS NOT AS FIXED AND INFLEXIBLE AS YOU THINK."

Scott Joplin Answers

1. What was the name of the HBCU I attended?
   A. Morehouse College
   B. George R. Smith College
   C. Howard University
2. What year did I publish Maple Leaf Rag?
   A. 1898
   B. 1897
   C. 1899
3. What was my nickname?
   A. King of Ragtime
   B. King of Swing
   C. King of Jazz

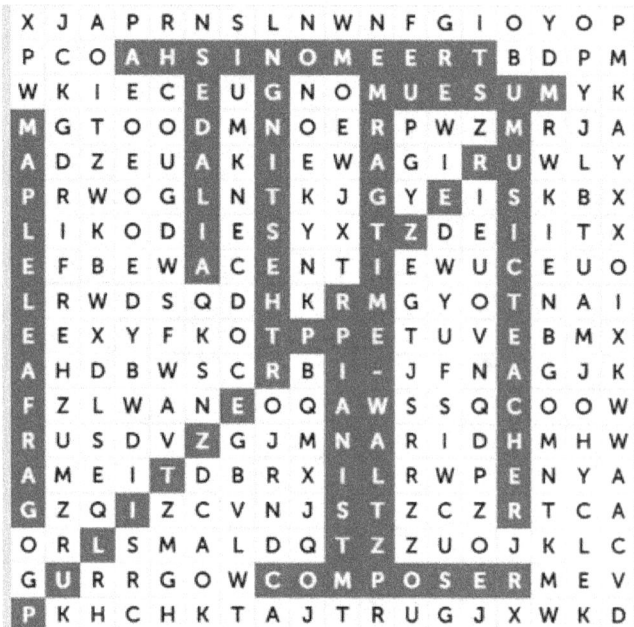

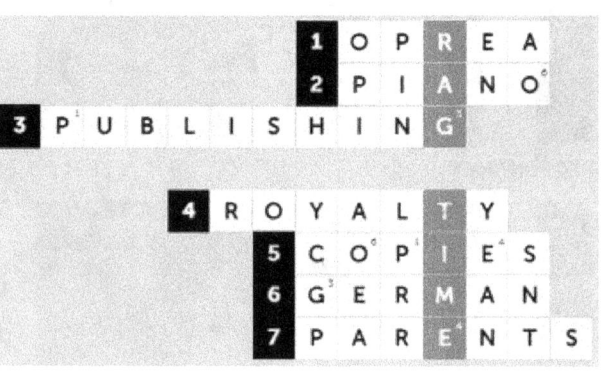

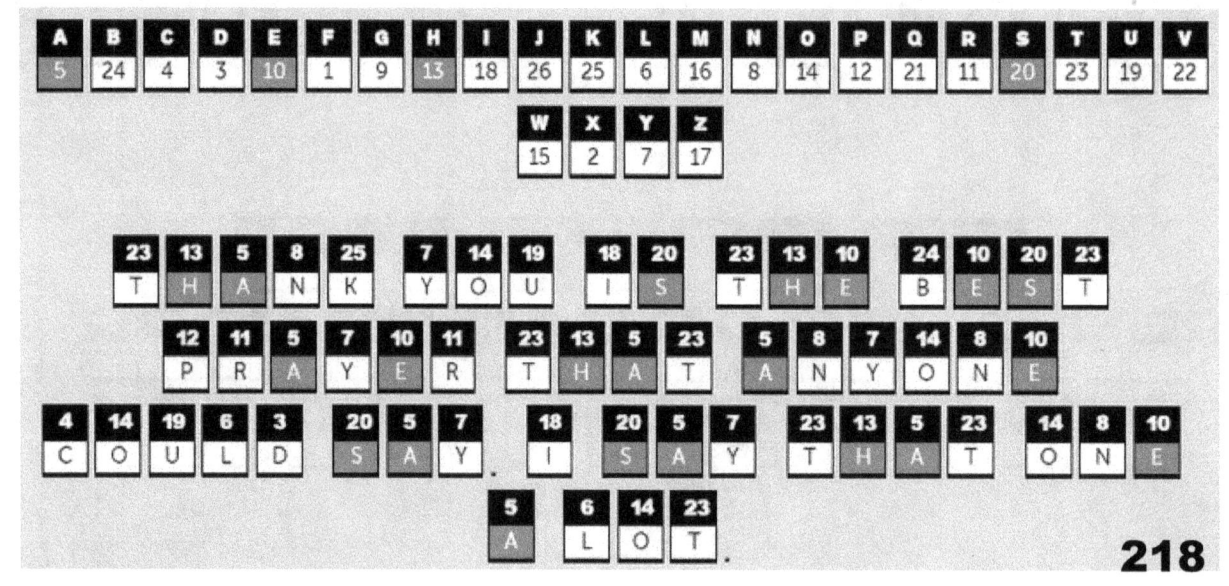

"THANK YOU IS THE BEST PRAYER THAT ANYONE COULD SAY. I SAY THAT ONE A LOT."

218

1. Which company didn't I model for?
   A. Macy's
   B. Old Navy
   C. Nordstrom
2. What is the name of my first Television show?
   A. Shake It Up
   B. Frenemies
   C. Dancing with the Stars
3. Which movie was my debut?
   A. Dune
   B. Spider-Man: Homecoming
   C. Smallfoot

Zendaya Coleman

Answers

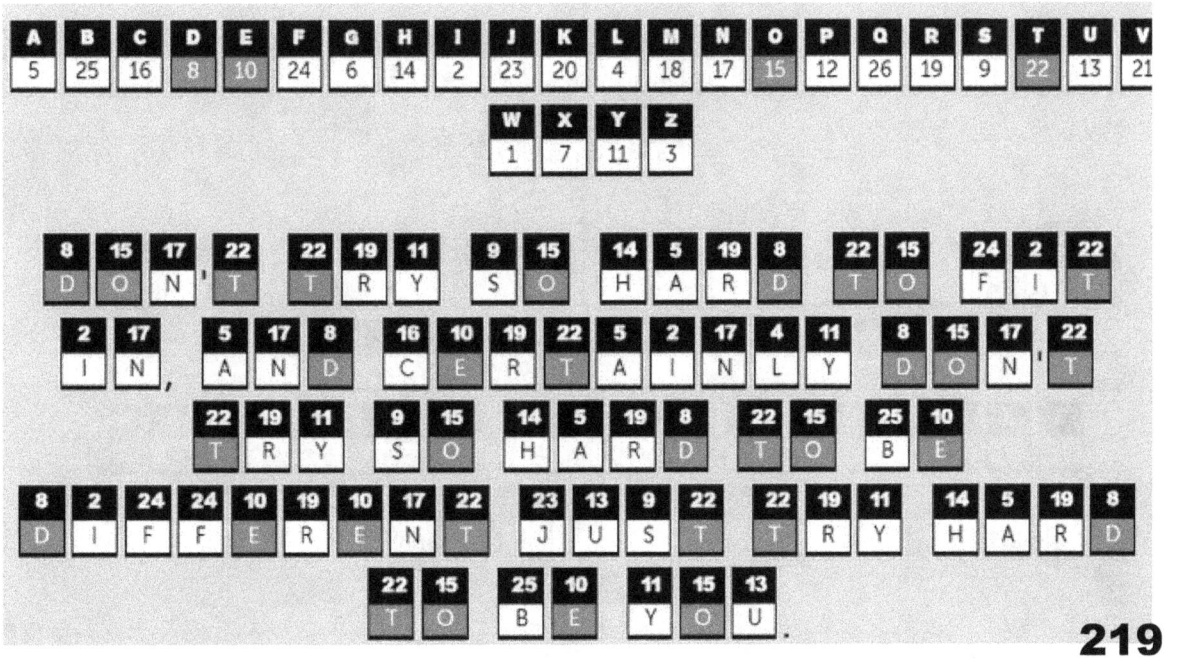

Levar Burton Answers

1. What was the name of the college I graduated from?
   A. University of Southern California
   B. University of South Carolina
   C. University of California
2. What year did I make my acting debut?
   A. 1977
   B. 1976
   C. 1983
3. I hosted and was the executive producer for what show?
   A. Mister Rogers' Neighborhood
   B. Jim Henson's Muppet Babies
   C. Reading Rainbow

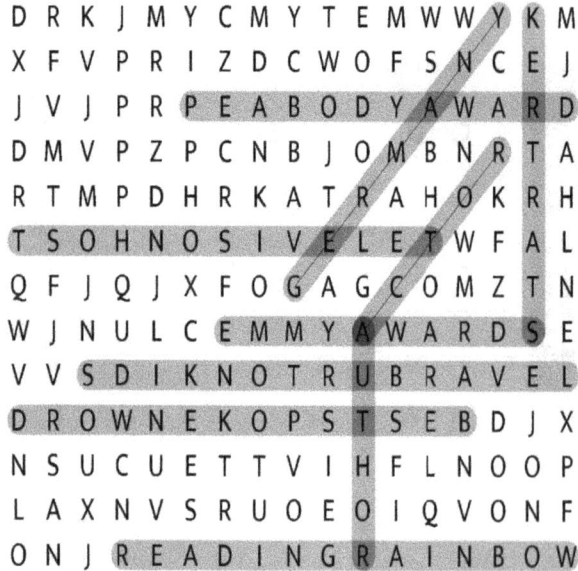

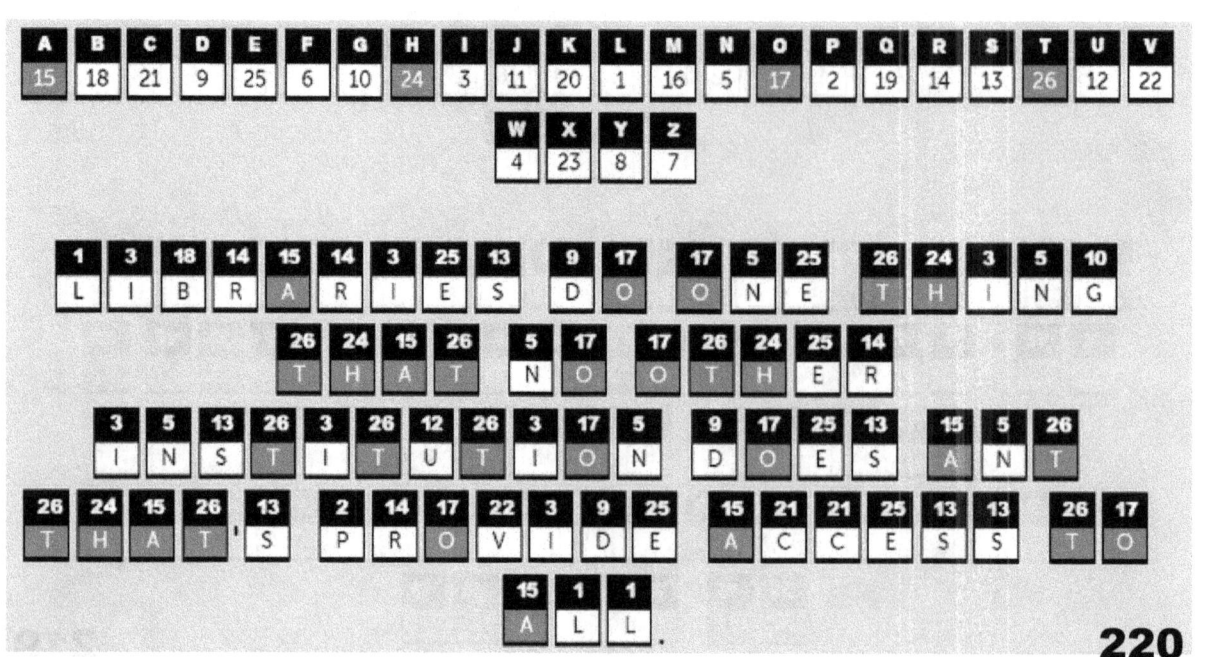

"LIBRARIES DO ONE THING THAT NO OTHER INSTITUTION DOES ANT THAT'S PROVIDE ACCESS TO ALL."

220

1. What was the name of the magazine I modeled for at 15?
   A. JET
   B. Ebony
   C. Time
2. What year did I make my film debut?
   A. 1961
   B. 1955
   C. 1954
3. I was the first African-American woman to win a?
   A. Tony Award for best actress
   B. Emmy Award for best actress
   C. Golden Globe Award for best actress

Carol Diann Johnson
Answers

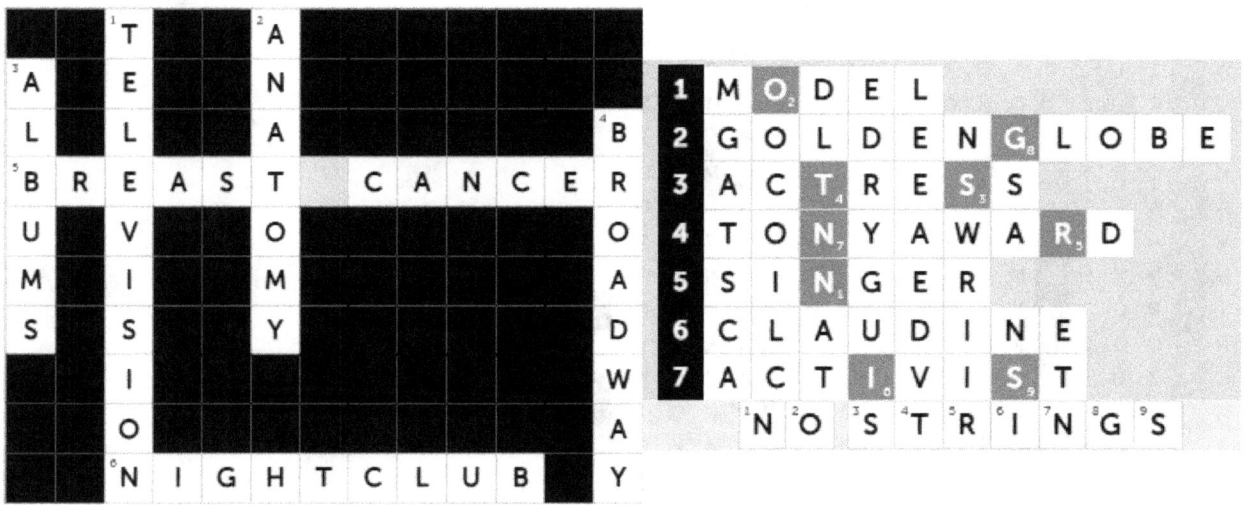

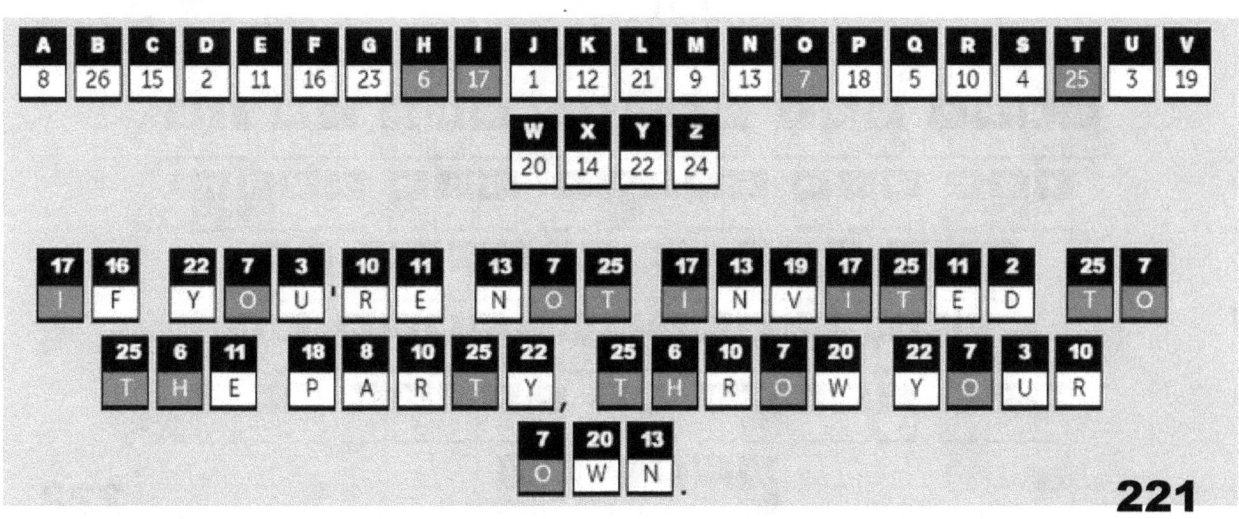

IF YOU'RE NOT INVITED TO THE PARTY, THROW YOUR OWN.

Harold Bellanfanti

Answers

1. What branch of the military did I serve in?
   A. Marine Corps
   B. Army
   C. Navy
2. What year did I start my singing career?
   A. 1949
   B. 1953
   C. 1959
3. I was the first Jamaican American to win?
   A. Oscar
   B. Emmy
   C. Golden Globe

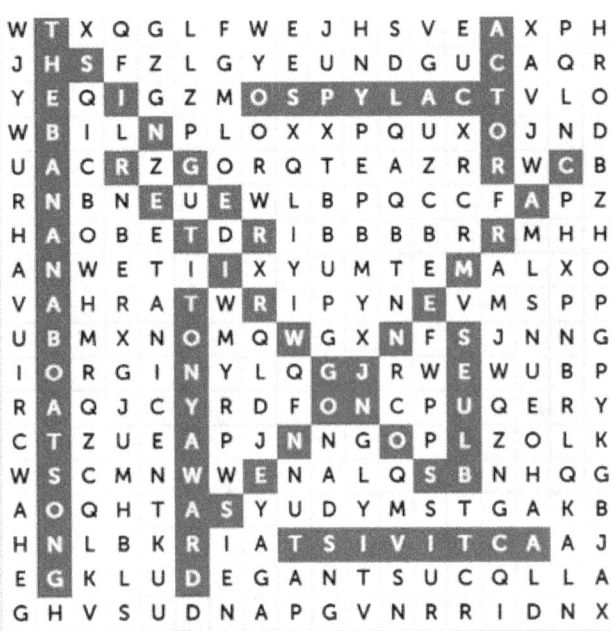

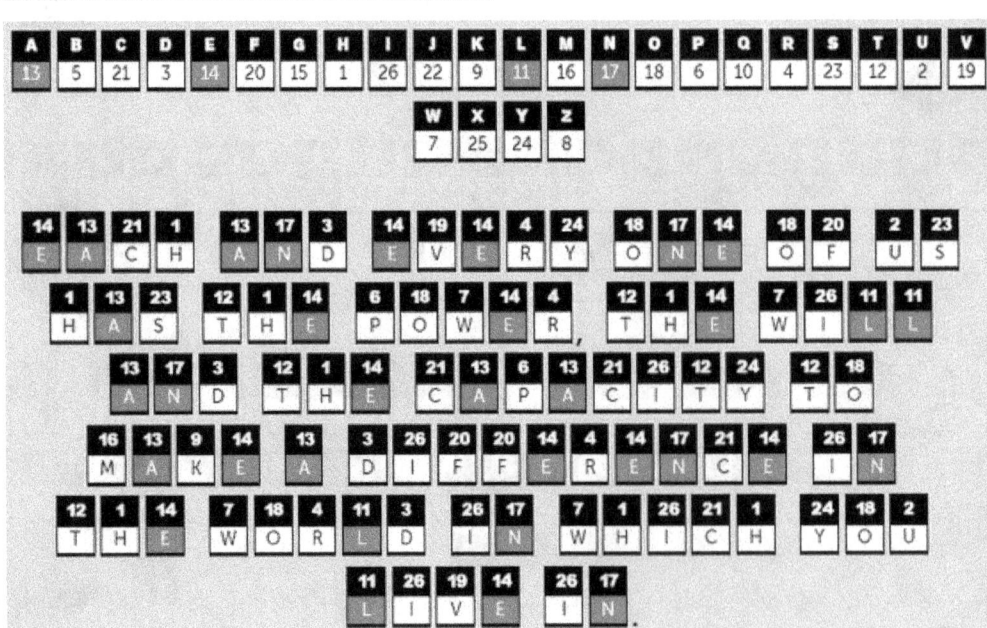

EACH AND EVERY ONE OF US
HAS THE POWER, THE WILL
AND THE CAPACITY TO
MAKE A DIFFERENCE IN
THE WORLD IN WHICH YOU
LIVE IN.

222

1. What is the name of the college I went to?
   A. Harvard University
   B. Yale University
   C. Berkeley University
2. What year did I debut in films?
   A. 1986
   B. 1985
   C. 1991
3. In Malcolm X I played the role of?
   A. Ramonda
   B. Betty Shabazz
   C. Tina Turner

Angela Bassett
Answers

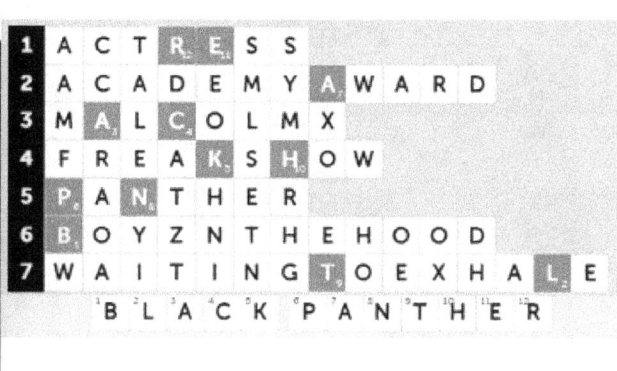

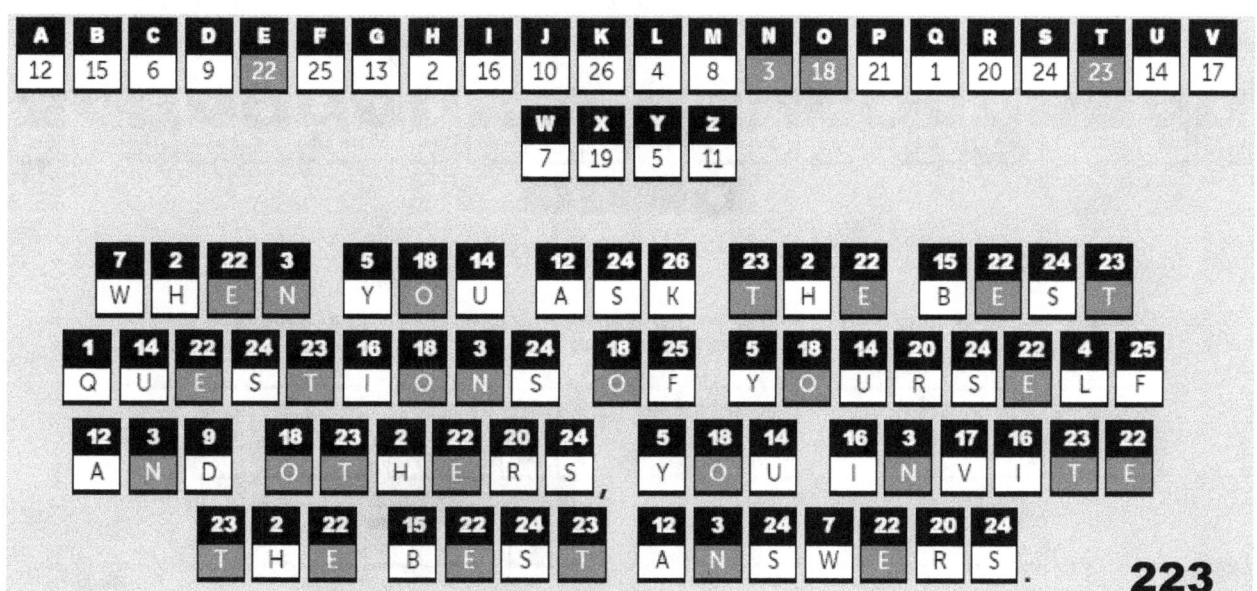

"WHEN YOU ASK THE BEST QUESTIONS OF YOURSELF AND OTHERS, YOU INVITE THE BEST ANSWERS."

223

1. What is the name of my fraternity?
   A. Omega Psi Phi
   B. Alpha Phi Alpha
   C. Kappa Alpha Psi
2. What film was my debut into Hollywood?
   A. Poetic Justice
   B. Boyz n the Hood
   C. 2 Fast 2 Furious
3. I was the youngest person ever nominated for?
   A. Best Director
   B. Best Actor
   C. Best Supporting Actor

John Singleton
Answers

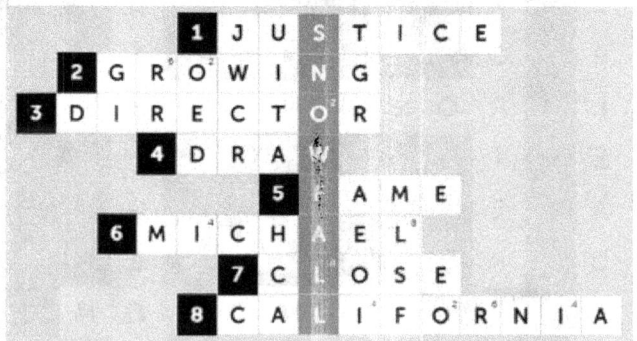
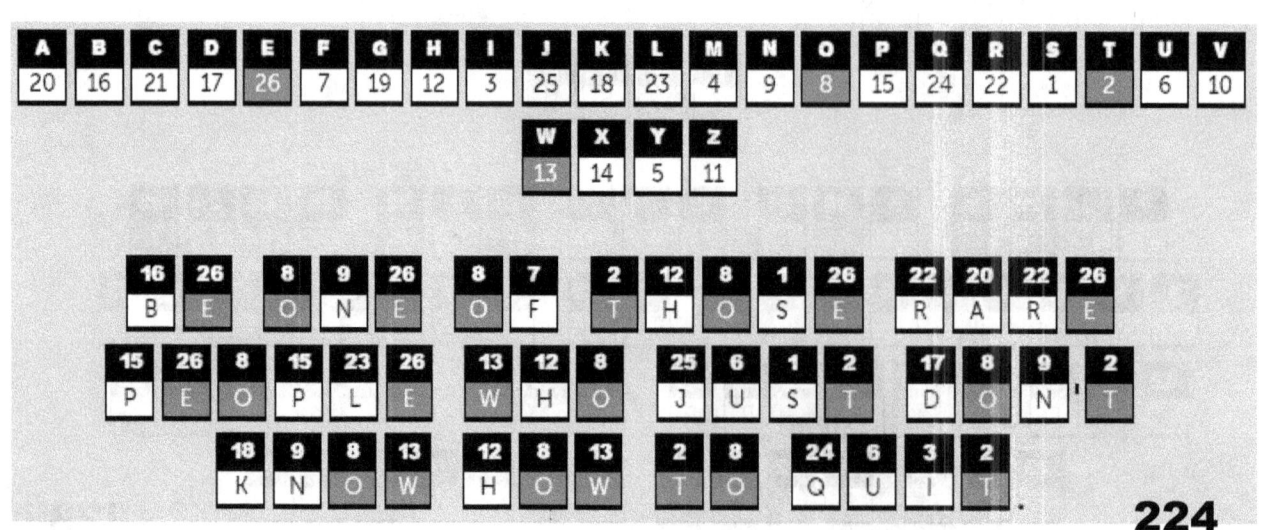

BE ONE OF THOSE RARE PEOPLE WHO JUST DON'T KNOW HOW TO QUIT.

224

Viola Davis Answers

1. What Performing Arts school did I attend?
   A. NYU Tisch School of the Arts—Drama and Dance
   B. The Juilliard School—Drama and Dance
   C. UNC School of the Arts—Drama and Dance
2. What year did I make my debut in film?
   A. 1996
   B. 1992
   C. 2011
3. In 2020 I became the most-nominated black actress in?
   A. Emmy history
   B. Golden Globe history
   C. Oscar history

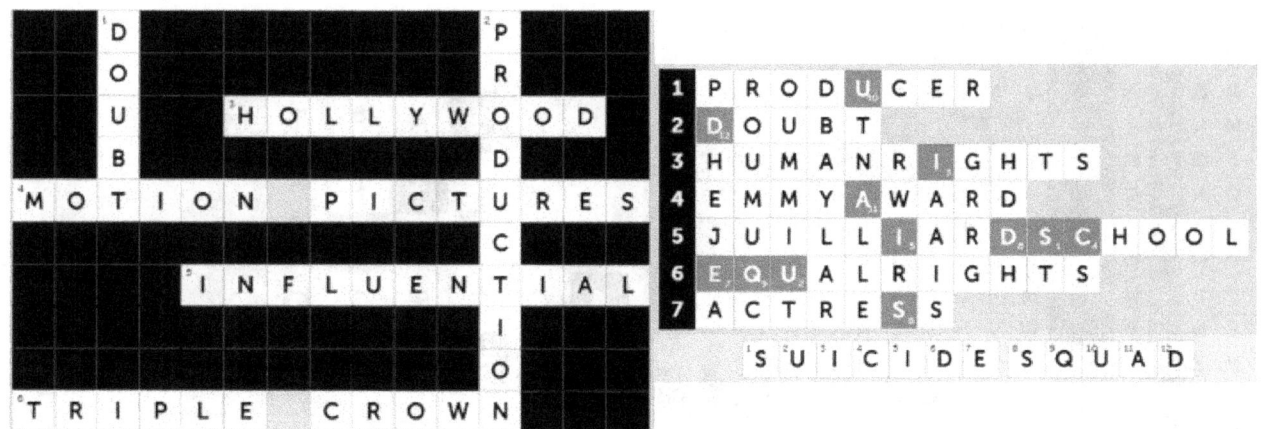

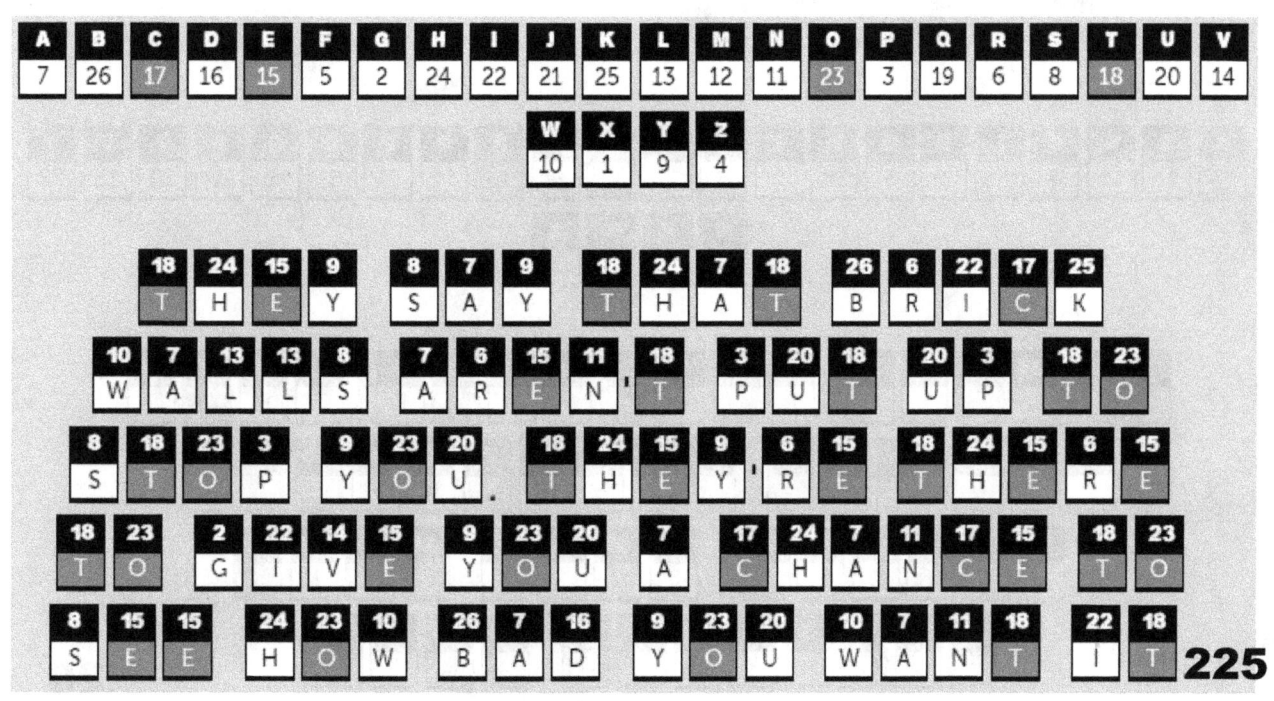

"THEY SAY THAT BRICK WALLS AREN'T PUT UP TO STOP YOU. THEY'RE THERE TO GIVE YOU A CHANCE TO SEE HOW BAD YOU WANT IT"

Cabell Calloway
Answers

1. Who taught me how to sing in scat style?
   A. Duke Ellington
   B. Betty Boop
   C. Louis Armstrong
2. I was the first African American to have a?
   A. Record Deal
   B. Nationally Syndicated Radio Show
   C. My own Orchestra
3. My Song Minnie the Moocher was the first single record?
   A. To sell a million copies
   B. To reach #1 on the Billboard 100
   C. To be used in a cartoon

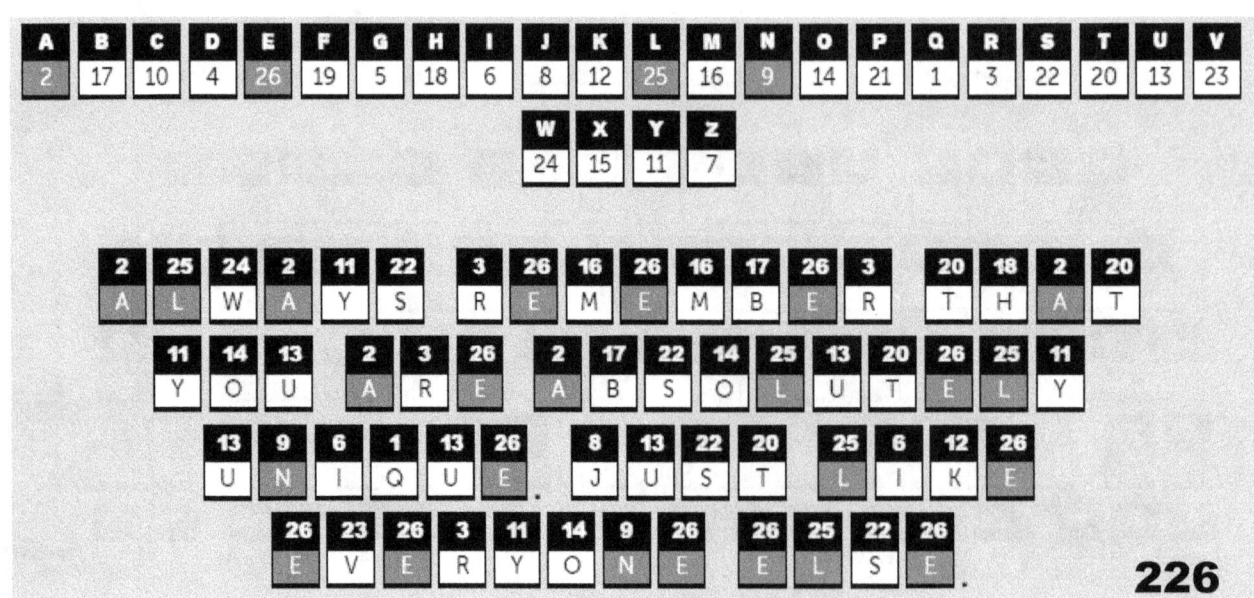

ALWAYS REMEMBER THAT YOU ARE ABSOLUTELY UNIQUE. JUST LIKE EVERYONE ELSE.

226

1. Our group name before The Dandridge Sisters was?
   A. The Wonder Children
   B. The Wonder Kids
   C. The Wonder Sisters
2. What year did I make my film debut?
   A. 1934
   B. 1935
   C. 1936
3. I was the first African American nominated for?
   A. Golden Globe for Best Actress
   B. Academy Award for Best Actress
   C. Emmy for Best Actress

Dorothy Dandridge
Answers

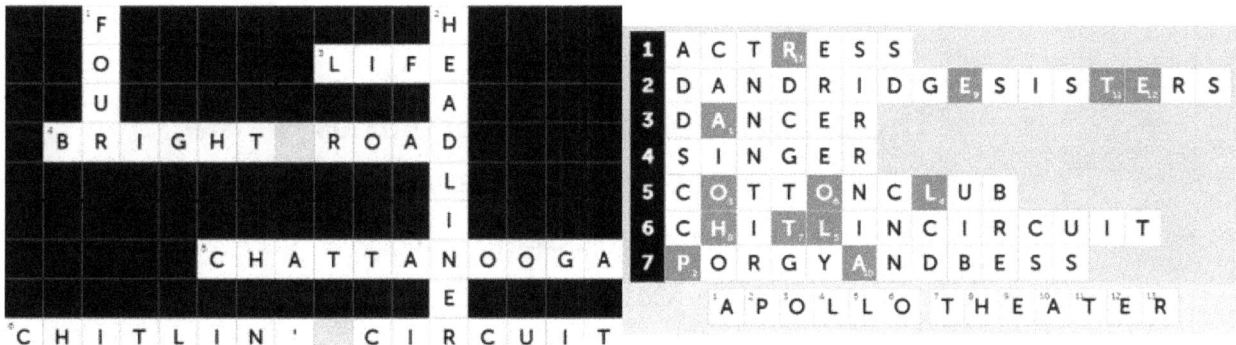

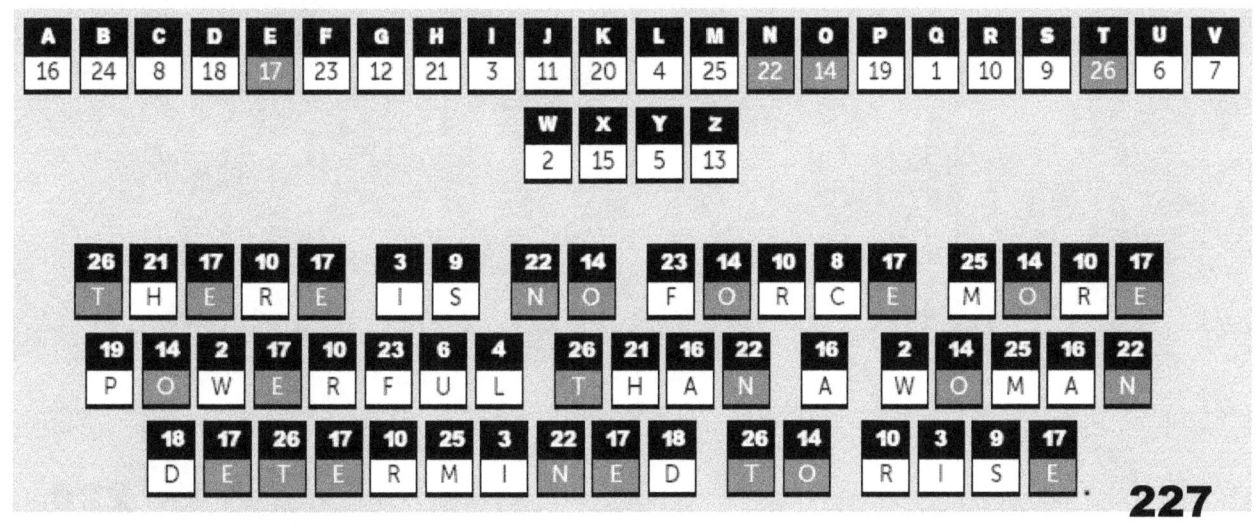

"THERE IS NO FORCE MORE POWERFUL THAN A WOMAN DETERMINED TO RISE."

Answers to all questions and puzzles in order of the table of contents.

This book is dedicated to my grandkids
Anais Isabella Pablo-Antonio
Deyshawn Frank Chambers
Alicia Marie Jackson
Ayianna Marie Chambers
Zion Jamaris Jackson
Jayvon Jerome Jackson

ABOUT THE AUTHOR

Matthew D. Hale, the author of Black Historical Figures is a retired Marine and disabled veteran. He received his Bachelor of Arts in Computer Science from Campbell University and his Master of Science in Computer Engineering from Boston University. Matthew spends his down time making music, traveling, playing, and developing his own video games. Follow Matthew on Facebook/Meta at wegonnalearntoday, Instagram @ w_g_l_t and Tic Tok at wegonnalearntoday. Go to wegonnalearntoday.com or everydollarcountz.com for additional information.

In 2020 Matthew developed an interactive website, www.wegonnalearntoday, to provide access to Black History through games, music and videos. The website grew into the Black Historical Figures workbook series as a way to supplement the black history curricula taught in the school systems.

'In order to grow you must visit uncomfortable places'

10 BOOK SERIES
RELEASE DATES

NOVEMBER 2022

FEBRUARY 2023

MAY 2023

AUGUST 2023

NOVEMBER 2023

GET YOUR COPY TODAY
DON'T FORGET TO TELL A FRIEND

www.ingramcontent.com/pod-product-compliance
Lightning Source LLC
Chambersburg PA
CBHW080335170426
43194CB00014B/2568